EXPLORING CAREERS USING FOREIGN LANGUAGES

EXPLORING CAREERS USING FOREIGN LANGUAGES

By
E.W. Edwards

THE ROSEN PUBLISHING GROUP, INC.
New York

Published in 1982, 1983, 1990 by the Rosen Publishing Group, Inc.
29 East 21st Street, New York, N.Y. 10010

Revised Edition 1990

Manufactured in the United States of America.

Library of Congress Cataloging-in-Publication Data

Edwards, E. W., 1945–
    Exploring careers using foreign languages.

    (Careers in depth)
    1. Language and languages—Vocational guidance—United States   I. Title.
II. Series.   P60.E37   402.3′731   81-22673
ISBN 0-8239-0968-9   AACR2

Contents

Preface to the Revised Edition

When starting to learn a foreign language, one dreads the onerous task of mechanical repetition, which reduces the student to a mere parrot. Yet because each language is ultimately a set of expressions that have evolved through usage, often there is no way to acquire a language but memorization. Once this initial hurdle is passed, however, a foreign language can be one's ticket to a new identity, leading to a greater empathy with peoples and their various means of cultural expression. Although there may be a universal language that is none other than human understanding, the fact is that we cannot deny the multitude of cultures on our planet, nor overlook their differences in outlook. In this book you will be informed about the practical applications of learning a foreign language. We will show you the exciting spectrum of careers to be had once you master the language of your choice.

The world is growing smaller because of the technological advances in communications. Yet real communication is not made of telephone circuits and computer chips; it is achieved by the human intellect that uses language as a tool for the exchange of information.

Not only is the rest of the world coming into contact with America, but equally the very nature of the American landscape is changing in more than the literal sense. The influence of foreign cultures and industries is as immediate as the car in your driveway or the shoes on your feet. We cannot be other than international.

The opportunities provided by this phenomenon are not without special difficulties. If you master a language and seek to understand the culture that produced it, you will begin to see the potential problems that cultures encounter when trying to communicate with each other. For example, characters in the Chinese language today are the same ones that date as far back as 200 B.C. At scientific and academic conferences with Western participants it is very difficult to render modern technological jargon into translation. Because Chinese is not a language constructed from an alphabet, one cannot simply invent new words. In such case, an interpreter or translator would have to use the correct English term within the grammatical context of the Chinese language.

Since the first edition of this book, we have not changed our opinion that indeed the world is getting to be a smaller place. However, we thought it might be helpful to add a chapter dealing with three key regions that are at the forefront of American interests because of the economic transformations occurring in them: Western Europe, the Soviet Union, and the Pacific Rim. We have chosen these regions not to exclude the rest of the world as culturally insignificant, but rather to discuss how these economic changes will lead to potential careers that require the command of a commonly used foreign language.

Introduction

Parla italiano? Sprechen Sie Deutsch? Habla español? Parlez-vous français? Maybe you can speak and write all of these languages. Maybe only one. Maybe you know Russian and Chinese. Maybe you've just finished your first week of basic Arabic. Whatever your language or languages, whatever your current degree of proficiency, if you want to know how your knowledge of a foreign language can be turned into a full and satisfying career or how this knowledge can be a tremendous asset in various other professions, then keep reading.

The world is a big place, but it's getting smaller. Rapid transport, mass communication, waves of immigration are all factors that contribute in large part to the linkage of opposite ends of the earth. Thirty years ago, traveling on a prop plane, it took sixteen hours to fly to Europe, and even then few could afford to go. Now, groups of vacationers set off for the Costa del Sol in Spain or the Swiss Alps for a week's vacation at a price they can afford, and it takes them only six hours to get there. Abroad, they are exposed to new scenery, customs, foods, and languages. Businessmen with interests in different parts of the world have taken to flying many thousands of miles for a day's conference or a two-day sales meeting. The Concorde, that marvel of Anglo-French engineering, can fly a person from London to New York in three hours. Politicians in their quest for solutions to difficult world problems engage in "shuttle diplomacy," flying to six countries in as many days with their proposals, pacts, and treaties.

Of course, even if you don't travel, you're still never really cut off from the rest of the world; television and radio bring it to you. You're as far away from China or South Africa as the distance from your armchair to the "on" switch of your television or radio set. News comes pouring in. Roving TV camera crews bring you on-the-spot coverage. If you possess an especially strong short-wave radio set, you can pick up the BBC World Service from London as well as broadcasts from many other countries in many languages. Through our own overseas service, the Voice of America, the United States sends broadcasts abroad. And let us not forget the service that newspapers and magazines provide in the dissemination of information: feature stories with accompanying photographs about such diverse places as Mozambique, Australia, and Finland, for example. In most of the urban centers of the United States there are newsstands that carry periodicals from all over the world. Undoubtedly you'll find *Corriere della Sera* from Milan, *Pravda* from Moscow, *The Times* from London, *Le Monde* from Paris. For varying amounts above the publication price in the country of origin, you can get a daily paper that is at most a few days old. In some cases the newspaper arrives on the very same day. As they say: "News travels fast."

Who reads all these foreign papers? That question brings us to the third important element involved in our perception of the world as a smaller place. Due to political or religious oppression, economic hardships, war, and a number of less terrible forces, people do not always remain in the country where they were born. The desire to live someplace else in the hope of having a better life has motivated Jews to emigrate to Israel, Englishmen to Australia, and Russians to France, to name but a few. Of all countries, the United States perhaps has the greatest reputation as a haven for immigrants. Indeed, ours is a country of immigrants, the only native Americans being the American Indians. We have all learned in history class about the unique contributions that different ethnic groups have made to this country. The scope of this book does not allow for a lengthy discussion of them. Suffice it to say that when the people of an ethnic or national group settle in this country, or any other for that matter, they are not stricken with instant amnesia, which is to say that they do not forget the language and customs of their native land. Often their feelings of identification with that land are all the stronger for being away from it. Admittedly there is a gradual process of assimi-

lation, usually affecting the second, third, and subsequent generations, but for the first generation and later generations interested in
their heritage, their "roots," the desire to be a small part of the
place from which they came is a very real concern. These people
form a part of the readership of the periodicals from abroad. Of
course, there are also the many travelers who want news from home.
In some cases, particularly for new residents of this country living
together in communities of their own, people who have not yet
mastered the rudiments of English, the news contained in periodicals
from abroad is not enough. These people usually want information
about the communities in which they're living, news relevant to
their daily lives. Out of such a need have sprung foreign-language
newspapers written and printed in the United States. Dealing largely
with domestic and community news, these papers are still another
testament to the great diversity of languages being used in this
country, a further indication of how languages have crossed national
boundaries and made distant places seem next door.

The whole question of foreign languages and the mass media will
be dealt with in Chapter VI. For the moment, let us confine ourselves
to the facts that in the United States numerous languages are spoken
and that the opportunities for a person with a good working knowledge of another language are many. We shall see that employment
in this field need not be limited to working in the United States.
American companies with offices abroad are constantly on the lookout for people with languages who will be able to function efficiently
in those branch offices. The American government both at home
and abroad is a major employer of people competent in other languages. The whole world of diplomacy is one in which the need for
dialogue is crucial. In order to hold a dialogue it is necessary to be
able to communicate, and in order to communicate it is necessary
to understand and be understood. Translators and interpreters are
vital for this purpose. As we all know, there is much paperwork in
government. If we only consider how much paper must move around
the world between governments, we can get some idea of how large
and necessary a task it is to render those documents into the appropriate language. The same holds true in the world of commerce, the

world of ideas, the world of travel. And it's not just a question of paperwork; in all of these worlds there are personal dealings in which the spoken word is the medium of communication. (Herein lies the distinction between the interpreter and the translator. The translator renders the written words — and by extension the sentences and paragraphs — of one language into a written form so that it makes sense in another language. The interpreter does the same thing with the spoken word.) You can safely assume, then, that in whatever field of endeavor your interests or talents lie, if that field is worldwide in either scope or purpose, there is a place for a multilingual person.

With any job, when you're trying to determine whether or not it is suitable for you, one of the best things you can do, and also one of the first, is to try to look at yourself objectively. "What kind of person am I?" you might ask yourself. "Do I like to be with people or do I prefer to do things by myself?" "Am I self-disciplined or do I need someone to tell me what to do?" "Do I want to make a lot of money or am I content with little?" "Do I want to keep regular office hours or do I like to work at varied hours through the day and night?" Establish criteria. Set yourself guidelines and goals. From the beginning you might as well try to find a job that matches your personal needs. Naturally, no job — unless it's one you create for yourself — will match all those needs entirely, but some positions will suit you better than others.

There is no one set of characteristics that a person working with foreign languages needs to possess. As has been indicated, the field is sufficiently broad to allow people with different temperaments to work in it. Specialties within the field, however, may be said to have certain temperamental prerequisites. For instance, persons who don't like to speak in public should not consider the field of interpreting; however, if they like reading and writing, translating might be just the thing. We shall go into all these particulars later. Generally speaking, people choosing careers using foreign languages should regard precision and accuracy as essential traits. They should be people who take the time and the trouble to get things right. In many foreign languages one vowel can mean the difference between a verb in the second person singular and in the third person singular, between past and present tense. You simply cannot afford to be sloppy. So bear in mind that dealing with foreign languages is an exacting discipline.

A more subtle characteristic of successful polyglots (persons who speak many languages) is an ability to surrender themselves; that is, a capacity to get outside of themselves in order to function better in another language. Other languages have other sets of rules; as is the case with any game, in order to play it you must adapt to the rules, because the rules won't adapt to you. It has been said, "When you speak another language, you live another life." Speaking and writing another language is not merely a matter of manipulating foreign words and structuring sentences to conform to a specific set of rules found in a book of grammar; it is a matter of entering another world, learning another mentality, another way of life. To do that effectively, you must be flexible, able to accept a number of different, often contradictory, ways of looking at the world. All this would suggest, then, that the person working with foreign languages should possess a deep curiosity about things new and different, a willingness to hold in abeyance the givens of his own upbringing, to withold judgment in an attempt to learn more fully, so that he or she will be at home living in another language.

Before we discuss the specific jobs available to those who speak languages, let us try to come to a clear understanding of what language is and how it works. To start with, we can say that language is one of the ways by which we communicate. Although language is not the only means through which we communicate—dance, body language, music, painting, and drawing are other means of expression—our initial definition does not suffer for not being exclusive. But by saying we communicate through language, we are really only saying how we use this thing called language; we have not said exactly what language *is*. Anthony Burgess, the famous author of *A Clockwork Orange,* in his book *Language Made Plain* says, " . . . language may be regarded as a link between a sound and a thought." Now, that helps a lot, for we are told one of the physical properties of language, that is, sound—just as if we were given one of the chemical components of a substance—and with that, its relation to an abstract, intangible process, that is, thought. It is not difficult to see the sort of deep waters we're now heading for. In defining things, one constantly seeks to define the words that have been used in the first effort to define the thing itself. Given this, it is evident that we will have to turn our thoughts to the nature of thought, the nature of sound. The entire complicated business is, in fact, the concern of the science called linguistics.

EXPLORING CAREERS USING FOREIGN LANGUAGES

Chapter **I**

Acquiring and Using Languages

Most of us are completely unaware of how we learned our native tongue. The sounds, stresses, and hesitations required to communicate words might almost have been born with us, so familiar are they from months and years of hearing them from our parents and other adults, from trial and error in our own baby days. But we did have to learn those sounds, and the learning process was basically one of imitation.

When it comes to learning a second language, not everyone is equally adept. Some of us have trouble making the different sounds required. Our tongue is accustomed to taking certain positions and can't seem to reproduce the hisses, rolled r's, and explosions of air required by the unfamiliar language. Some of us have trouble hearing the difference between certain sounds. Others can't grasp the unusual system of grammar, or word order, of tenses and word endings that do not occur in our native language.

Some people, on the other hand, have "an ear for languages." They have a gift that is similar to being able to play musical instruments by ear. The comparison to music is apt, because such people are often musical; sound is an integral part of language. Good linguists are also often good mimics; they can adopt a Scottish burr or an Irish brogue or a Swedish accent just by having had casual contact with speakers of those languages.

On the other hand, mimicry is not everything, and languages, like any other skill, can be learned by plain hard work. Persistence and determination to learn can go a long way in compensating for lack of natural ability.

The study of foreign languages in the United States usually begins in junior or senior high school; little language training occurs in elementary school. That is unfortunate, because small children usually learn languages with the greatest facility. Their speech habits are not yet firmly entrenched, and they find the addition of new sounds and words easier than do adults.

In foreign countries, the Netherlands and the Scandinavian countries have been particularly successful with language programs for children. It is not uncommon for fifteen-year-old Swedes to speak two or three languages fluently, having studied them for most of their school years. Those children, however, live in countries and a continent where borders are not between states, but between countries with totally "foreign" languages. In the United States, when we cross a border to do business or enjoy a vacation, our only language problem is likely to be a Southern or New England accent, which may be a novelty but is no barrier to communication.

In addition, the very size of the United States tends to isolate us linguistically. The distance from New York to California is more or less equivalent to the distance between Madrid and Moscow. We tend to think of the rest of the world in American terms: When we do travel outside our country, we may be amazed that the people don't speak English. The situation has changed somewhat with increasing waves of immigration from all parts of the world, bringing peoples who speak languages that are not even akin to English and the more familiar Romance languages of Europe. Nevertheless, viewing the country as a whole, insular attitudes still tend to prevail.

Language programs suffered in U.S. schools and colleges in the 1970's and early 1980's. The pervading philosophy behind the cuts in language programs seemed to be that the ability to conjugate the verbs to love, to walk, and to drink was not likely to get a student very far in the "real world." The view has some validity. The fault, however, does not lie with the entire discipline of language education, but rather with the quality and method of instruction. It's all well and good being able to translate the first lines of Dante's *Divine Comedy* from Italian into English, but if you can't ask "Where is the bathroom?" in Italian, something is wrong.

Modern languages exist as a means of communicating. Although the ability to read great literature in the original language is a great joy, for the beginning student that should be a goal to aspire to, not drudgery assigned for didactic purposes. Like children, we should be learning vocabulary to express immediate needs. Later can come the more complicated words and constructions that will enable us to communicate more complex feelings, to understand subtle, often purposely ambiguous, lines of poetry.

Happily, the trend in language teaching these past few years has been more along the lines of the practical approach. Students are encouraged to speak, and "real life" situations are often created in the classroom to force students to cope. Language learning is once again being viewed as important. Teachers and administrators recognize the growing necessity of being able to function on an international level in a world that is getting smaller. More languages are being offered in some schools. Some of the previous language requirements are coming back. Let's make sure, then, that yours will not become a generation of adults who go to parties and say, "I had four years of high school Russian, but, of course, I can't speak a word of it."

Whatever the nature of the language instruction, it should be stressed that the ultimate responsibility for learning lies with the pupil. Learning a language is just plain hard work. The words and forms must be memorized; no amount of special aids, electronic or otherwise, can replace study. Courses that guarantee to have you speaking French like a diplomat in two weeks are shams.

So make the most of the language classes that are offered to you. Study the lessons. Do the exercises in the textbook. Most important, perhaps, don't be shy in class. Take every opportunity to speak the language that is offered to you. If you should have a chance to study for a year in the country whose language you are learning, seize it. There is no better way to become fluent in a language than to live that language twenty-four hours a day.

If such a bonanza does not come your way, and you are confined to the classroom of your home town, there are still many ways to practice and improve your skills. Go to foreign films. Seek out native speakers of the language in your community; usually they are pleased to speak it and are delighted to help someone who is learning it. You might even be able to work out an exchange: English lessons for lessons in their language.

Collaborate with your classmates in ways to further your fluency. Go to ethnic restaurants and speak nothing but the language of the country. Place your order in that language. Chat with the owner.

For your written skills, try to find a pen pal with whom you can correspond in the language you're learning. You'll be amazed at the progress you can make when you are using the language for a purpose.

Bilingualism

People who have been brought up bilingually, speaking two languages at home, have a tremendous advantage, which should be exploited as much as possible. Frequently children from bilingual homes allow English to become their language of choice and use the second language less and less, principally in communicating with their family. This is a sad mistake and is like deliberately throwing away a birthright.

Children from bilingual homes sometimes speak perfectly but have difficulty in reading and writing. Those are skills that can be acquired in the classroom—just as they would have done had they been reared in the country of their parents' origin. But they are skills that will be essential in any career you undertake; don't be overconfident. Sloppiness will not be tolerated in professional surroundings.

Another factor to be borne in mind is that the foreign language spoken in your home may be a dialect of the language you're studying. A dialect differs from a regional accent in that not only sounds may be different, but also words and grammatical constructions. It would not be unusual in New York, for example, to find students in an Italian class who speak Sicilian at home, or students in a Spanish class who know Puerto Rican Spanish, but not Castilian.

Dialects are neither good nor bad; indeed, it is inappropriate to place any value judgment on them. Dialects exist and are used; they are the means by which certain people communicate. The links between dialects and class and other socioeconomic considerations are beyond the scope of this book. For our purposes, let us merely recognize that the standard form of a language—the body of words, for instance, contained in a standard dictionary of that language—is the form that a professional translator or interpreter will be called upon to use. It is the language of business, international conferences, and correspondence. Dialects may be thought of as regional, not a presence on the international stage. If a dialect is spoken in your home, it will doubtless help you in learning the standard form of the language, but don't make the mistake of considering the one a substitute for the other.

If the use of language is a career goal, the more languages you speak the better. If you are approaching mastery of one language, think about undertaking courses in another. Language classes in high school will give you background for the courses you will take in college at an institute for translators. Most American colleges and universities offer four-year bachelor of arts degrees in foreign languages. A language major usually entails about thirty-two credit hours in the language and about twelve credit hours of a related subject, which may well be another language. Spanish majors, for instance, may study Portuguese; Russian majors, Polish. After four years of language at a good university, you're well on your way to being prepared to enter the professional field.

Earning a Living with Languages

Depending on where you're situated geographically in this country, your level of competence in the foreign language or languages with which you'll be working, the language itself, and your own flexibility regarding the where, when, and what of your work, your chances of finding a job using the languages you know are generally pretty good. Jobs are available as translators and interpreters in business, in international organizations, and in government, not to mention all the language teaching jobs in and outside of academia. As with all jobs, a lot depends on you. Being a brilliant linguist is not always enough. Your work habits must be such as to inspire confidence in your employers. Being unable to meet deadlines will disqualify you for many positions that might otherwise have been open to you.

Obviously, where you decide to live will be a great factor in the number of jobs that will be available to you. It's safe to say that New York City offers the most opportunities. The United Nations alone generates an incredible amount of activity in the field of foreign languages. Whether or not you're working for the U.N. in some capacity (those jobs are discussed in Chapter III), the huge aggregation of foreigners necessarily drawn to that organization means that the services of speakers of other languages is in constant demand: free-lance translators and interpreters, tour guides, secretaries, chauffeurs, perhaps even bilingual bodyguards. Further, the fact that New York is the media capital of this country signifies that there will be openings for people with languages in publishing, radio, and television. Writers like to stay near New York because it allows them to keep in close contact with their agents and editors. The same is true of professional translators, who often rely on commissions from specific agencies or publishing houses. Contacts are important, especially when you're free-lance. Although, admittedly, one could translate a book anywhere—perhaps even working better in splendid isolation away from the hustle and bustle—to get the work to begin with it's best to be near where the work originates.

That is not to say that New York is the only place where you can use your other languages to good advantage. If you're interested in film, California is probably the place to be. If your heart is set on working for the federal government, you'll probably wind up spending a good part of your time in and around Washington. These are some of the realities behind the type of work you've chosen. Montana and Wyoming, for example, beautiful as they may be, will not provide the international atmosphere or the opportunities necessary for working with foreign languages.

Clearly, to get a good job, you have to be good at what you do. What exactly constitutes competence in another language? That largely depends upon what you'll be doing, but generally one can say that your knowledge of the other language should be more or less on a par with that of an educated native speaker. If you're translating, your written skills must be especially good both in your own language and the language into which you're translating. Interpreting demands exceptional fluency as well as an ability to shift rapidly from one language to another. Both disciplines require a sensitivity to words so that meanings in the two languages correspond as closely as possible. As a rule, four years of intensive language study ought to bring you up to this level. Ten years of intermittent contact and study of a language might be sufficient training as well. In addition to the actual linguistic competence outlined above, there is also the necessity to be well versed in the subject matter you're dealing with. This is crucial when the material is of a technical nature, material that someone with a general liberal arts education such as you'll probably receive will find foreign in itself. Whenever there is any doubt about a subject, whether in business or science or literature, it is necessary to confront it, take the trouble to familiarize yourself with the material through research or personal queries, and become competent in that subject.

Another factor that will determine whether or not you get a job using the language you know is the language itself. This pertains, as do most things in life, to the ever-present economic law of supply and demand. Is there a need for the language services you're offering? Are many people offering the same services? People with certain languages are in constant demand because so few people are proficient in those languages. For example, students who are proficient in Chinese will be in much greater demand than in previous years. The same might be said of Arabic and Russian. While there is a great volume of work available in Spanish, French, and other Romance languages, there are also large numbers of qualified people available to do the work. More exotic languages do not as a rule provide the same volume of work, but there are also not as many qualified people, and the need for qualified people is growing ever greater. That fact should play a part in your thinking about the languages you intend to study at the university. It should not, however, be your primary consideration. Given that you will be living with the languages you study for a long time to come, it is of the utmost importance that you be deeply interested in them, and being interested in a language also means being concerned with the customs, habits, literature, music, and art of the people whose language it is.

The last point worth mentioning in regard to finding a job is the matter of your own flexibility when confronted with choices in the marketplace of work. There are innumerable ways in which you might find yourself using your skills, ways perhaps that at this point you can't imagine. That being the case, it's important to look for work with an open mind. Some broadcasting jobs will require that you work certain nights, shift work. Various administrative jobs in business will require that you type. Try not to be put off by aspects of a job that at first sight don't seem particularly appealing. At least in the beginning, you should accommodate yourself as much as possible to the demands of the job. Later, after you've had more experience, you can start thinking about something that suits your needs more exactly. One can, of course, avoid the more onerous tasks of a 9-to-5 job by working free-lance. Here too, however, you must be flexible, because, the nature of free-lance work is very much feast or famine; that is to say, there's usually either a lot of work available or very little. Sometimes you will be working on something that was needed yesterday; all your other activities will have to be put aside until the task at hand is completed. Sometimes three pieces of work will be due on the same day. Sometimes you'll have all the time in the world and nothing to do. This sort of thing requires that you be able to shift and change your schedule accordingly.

Let's look now at some of the jobs that may be available to you as one proficient in another language. Let's talk about some of the things you ought to be thinking about when you review them.

The Different Jobs—Secretary to Spy

Knowledge of another language can give an added dimension to all sorts of jobs. If you enjoy using the language you know and your job gives you ample opportunity to use your skills, chances are you will be happy doing what you're doing.

The range of jobs in which language abilities are needed is broad. You can be a secretary or a spy. The choice is very much up to you. Know, however, what you're getting into. James Bond may be a very appealing figure on the silver screen, but the realities behind work in government intelligence will probably not conform with the image in your mind's eye. The following chapters will try to give you a good idea of what various jobs are like. Right now, let's look over a list of professions. A traditional field for people with languages is teaching. Those who have learned something that other people want to know can always teach. Knowledge in this sense is a very saleable commodity. There are many levels at which you can teach: you could be a university professor, a high school teacher, a teacher at a private language school, or a private tutor. It depends almost entirely on your qualifications, although personal inclination and the availability of positions are two factors that must, of course, be dealt with.

The most obvious work for a person with other languages is in translating and interpreting. Many of the jobs we shall discuss require that you translate and interpret as a part of many duties. There are, however, professional translators and interpreters who do nothing but that. The two disciplines are usually practiced separately, but not always and depending upon your talents needn't be. The largest employers of translators and interpreters are international organizations such as the United Nations (UN), the World Health Organization (WHO), and the United Nations Educational, Scientific, and Cultural Organization (UNESCO). The representatives of many nations who attend the conferences sponsored by these organizations must be able to communicate with one another, to know what's happening as it happens, to maintain the meaningful dialogue for which the conference was assembled. The staff translators and interpreters make all that happen. The conferences are held all over the world and deal with a variety of issues. The worldwide nature of the organizations creates for the staff member the possibility of being stationed in many places around the world as well as the opportunity to travel to cities where conferences are taking place. The same work can be done on a free-lance basis, but usually people who do so are former members of a staff and therefore have the necessary connections to be successful working on their own.

Regarding other jobs that involve translating and interpreting, positions exist in business, government, the media, law, science, social work, and many other areas. Within these fields, of course, some jobs require a greater or lesser degree of skill in an area outside of translating and interpreting. In business, for instance, working as a translator or interpreter might also require certain secretarial, or perhaps managerial, skills. In social work, an interpreter might also be a caseworker.

Knowledge of another language can be put to use in the above-mentioned fields not only by practicing translating and interpreting. Being able to conduct your everyday affairs in a second or third or fourth language, given the task at hand, can greatly facilitate your work. Consider the journalist covering a story abroad; trying to find out what's going on in Cairo without a knowledge of Arabic is a difficult proposition at best. The foreign correspondent who does not know the language of the country he's covering is reduced to relying in large part on official releases from government, business, and individuals; that is, anyone who chooses to hold a press conference. The opportunity for investigative reporting is necessarily severely circumscribed. Consider the president of a large import-export company; his business necessitates dealing with both suppliers and customers abroad. A good measure of success in this business depends on a knowlege of the various markets, knowing what's made in the U.S. that is desired in Italy, for example, or that Spanish X is what everyone is clamoring for in Philadephia. This sort of expertise can be most easily acquired by having contacts abroad who can furnish the necessary information and handle the product. Knowing the language of the people you're dealing with is of inestimable importance in that it establishes good personal relationships as well as giving one insights into the country and its consumer needs. Eliminating the cost of intermediary people such as translators and interpreters (on business trips or meetings at the home office) makes for a more streamlined enterprise.

Think about yourself then. Come to terms with your limitations, realize the extent of your abilities. Consider what you want to do. See which job comes closest to your ideal. Narrow down the fields. Where do you want to be ten years down the line?

Chapter 11

Teaching Foreign Languages

Teaching can be one of the most rewarding of all professions. Sharing what one knows, watching students master new skills, learning from one's own students are all experiences that make for an exciting and stimulating work atmosphere. Language teaching is an especially fulfilling area in that one opens up to the student not only another language but an entire new way of looking at the world, an entire new world for that matter. The language teacher presents to his or her students new ways of communicating. In a world so full of misunderstanding, that is a very important contribution. Who knows in what fields a teacher's students may wind up, in what ways they might influence the course of human events. There is always present this incredible feeling of potential in one's students, a factor that contributes to the energy that can be generated in the environment of the classroom. You, as teacher, are important.

As in all teaching jobs, there are many different levels at which you can teach a foreign language. Different skills and qualifications are necessary for different levels. The first thing to think about in deciding which level is for you is the age group of the students you would most like to teach. You will not be teaching literature to first graders, nor will college students particularly appreciate being taught nursery rhymes. Teenagers in the classroom present their own special challenges and rewards. Pay and working hours also vary according to level. University professors do not work a 9-to-3 day. They teach a specified number of classroom hours a week, which leaves them time to carry on their own research. University salaries, depending on one's status, are usually higher than those at the secondary school level.

Interest in foreign language studies in the U.S. decreased during the 1970s. Statistics for 1981 show that the number of language teachers decreased by almost half since 1971. For that reason, many language teachers chose to work overseas, where universities, colleges, and secondary schools were seeking qualified English teachers. In the U.S. such programs as Teaching English as a Foreign Language (TEFL) became more widespread in the latter part of the 1970s. In the 1990s we can expect growth of interest in foreign languages as more and more Americans realize that to acquire language skills is tantamount to opening new doors in almost any career, be it in business, government, or any other field.

Junior and Senior High Schools

In the early 1980s about two thirds of foreign language teachers worked in junior and senior high schools. The National Education Association estimated that of 962,000 secondary teachers about 18,000 taught foreign languages. Currently, at the university level there is a demand for foreign language teachers as many students prepare to go abroad for studies. These language courses are usually taught by a native speaker. Conversely, many countries outside the U.S. are looking for qualified English teachers. If you want to practice your newly acquired language, you might try teaching English in the country of your choice. In Japan there are even programs that sponsor Americans with college degrees but no knowledge of Japanese to teach English.

The usual qualifications for teaching in junior or senior high schools are: a bachelor of arts degree with a major in one or two foreign languages or a major in one foreign language and a minor in another subject that the person could also teach; a teaching certificate from the state (which requires completion of some educational courses as well as a number of hours of practice teaching); and experience in the foreign country either in the form of travel or prolonged residence. Requirements for a position are determined by the school district.

Salary is determined by the local boards. Community boards negotiate budgets with city and state authorities and determine pay for teachers. Starting salaries therefore can vary greatly. Starting salaries range from $12,000 to $20,000. In one respect, new graduates sometimes have a better chance of getting a job than veteran teachers, since they're usually more willing to travel and to accept appreciably lower salaries. Budget-conscious school boards might well be more interested in an enthusiastic inexperienced teacher than in a veteran able to command a higher salary.

College or University

What is it like teaching at a junior college, college, or university? What qualifications do you need? Is it more difficult to find a job at this level than at the high school level? What is the meaning of "publish or perish"?

University and college positions are very desirable. There is great competition for posts, and with the U.S. population decreasing— there are fewer children eventually to become college students— fewer and fewer positions are available. Universities and colleges saw their heyday in the sixties. As a result of the postwar baby boom in the forties, enrollment in the sixties was bursting at the seams. The emphasis placed on the need for higher education during that period was remarkable. A subway poster campaign in New York said, "Don't be called boy all your life. Go to college." The result of this and other similar messages was to make universities expand, increase their faculties, and open new departments; and new colleges opened their doors around the country. This, of course, was great for PhD's looking for jobs. They were in demand.

This situation changed radically in the 1970s, when students enrollment and interest declined. Since 1980, however, about 10 million students have enrolled as undergraduates, creating an increase of 35 percent. In the 1990s a turnover is expected, as a generation of professors will be retiring. Still, you must realize that college and university teaching positions are greatly sought after. However, if you are persistent, talented, and willing to go anywhere, however, you should eventually land the teaching job you want.

Why is college teaching considered such a good job? One reason is the freedom. Depending on your level of seniority, you can create the classes you want to teach. If you have established your expertise in one subject that you are going to teach—such as seventeenth-century German poetry, for example—your professional research then is complemented by your lectures and seminars. What could be more satisfying for an academic than to teach and discuss the very subjects to which he or she has devoted scholarly interest and professional writing? College professors as a rule don't teach more than six hours a week. That doesn't mean that all the rest of their time is free, although many people who work nine-to-five jobs think so. Besides the many hours devoted to class preparation, professors are expected to do research in their areas of interest and expertise and to publish their findings and theories either in book form or as articles in scholarly journals. That brings up the matter of ''publish or perish,'' which is discussed later.

Another reason many students find the idea of a college teaching career appealing is the prestige the job carries. Professor is still a title of distinction, conferring on those who possess it the laurels of accomplishment. As a faculty member you will be expected to be extremely knowledgeable in certain specific areas of your discipline. The hope is that with time and study, experience and devotion, you will become an expert in your field. It is this possibility of becoming an authority in a given field that many students find particularly attractive about being a university or college professor. Some say that the teacher is really just another student, and in so far as he or she is always learning something new, that is true. The fact that university professors work on campuses surrounded by young people eager to learn makes them feel a part of a growing, maturing process and keeps them eternally young.

For those of us who look back on our university days as the best ones we had, it is clear why being a college professor seems like one of the best jobs a person could possibly have. Just think of all the wonderful films and concerts and lectures that are constantly presented on university campuses all over the country. In many places, especially when there is not a major urban center nearby, the college or university is the hub of intellectual life in the community. As a teacher there, you are at the heart of it all.

Another advantage worth considering is the scholarly community that surrounds you. What could be more congenial than to pass one's working life among people who share similar interests. Consorting with professors from other departments can be fascinating and rewarding in that one can learn so much. Some professors speak about a worldwide community of scholars and say that they never feel lonely no matter where they are, either in this country or abroad. Whether they have met many scholars at the conventions held by various societies from year to year, or whether they have come to know a scholar through his written work, if geography permits they can get together and discuss many subjects of common interest. Of course, the picture here painted is an ideal one. You mustn't get the impression that all college professors love one another. In fact, professional rivalry can cause some of the bitterest disputes imaginable. Nonetheless, the potential for finding a circle of interesting friends is perhaps greater in the university community than in any other.

The freedom afforded by a college teaching career was mentioned earlier. Besides the flexibility of the weekly teaching schedule, however, there is the vacation time the job allows. Here university teaching is unsurpassed by any other profession. A university professor is on the same academic timetable as his or her students, having Christmas vacation, usually three weeks; Easter vacation, usually one week; and summer vacation, usually three months if he or she does not choose to teach a summer session. Add to these holidays Thanksgiving and the national holidays, and you can see why some people wouldn't consider any other job. Sabbaticals, which are paid leaves of absence for faculty members with a certain number of years of teaching to their credit, are another appealing aspect of university life. Sabbaticals usually are for a year and allow professors to pursue their own research undisturbed.

What about salary? The College and University Personnel Association reports for 1984–85 that salaries for foreign language teachers in public and private colleges ranged from $18,000 to $36,000 depending on the teacher's position. National Education Association statistics show that women university teachers make between $1,000 and $1,500 less than men.

If one's work is published, there is the additional income from the royalties of one's books. Be realistic, however; unless you write a textbook that is adopted as a standard text for a course, there's not much money in scholarly publication. Articles written for scholarly journals earn the author no money at all, though the resulting exposure in academic circles can potentially be worth its weight in gold in that such articles are an important factor in whether or not you will be given a permanent position on the faculty. This permanent position, called tenure, will be explained when we discuss the qualifications for teaching at the various levels within the university hierarchy.

First let's look at the differences between a junior college, a college, and a university. A junior college has only a two-year curriculum and does not offer a bachelor's degree. A college, on the other hand, offers a four-year program leading to the BA or BS degree. A university differs from a college in that, in addition to offering undergraduate degrees, it also has a graduate school where students can study toward a master's degree and then toward a doctor's degree or PhD. These advanced degrees are important to bear in mind because even junior colleges usually require their staff to have at least a master's degree and only rarely will a college or university hire someone who does not have a PhD.

Here then is what you need to teach at college level. For junior college, a master's degree is usually necessary. Sometimes one must have completed or be working toward a doctorate, and sometimes a teaching certificate is required. To gain a position on the staff at a college, it is necessary either to have a PhD or to be completing a doctoral dissertation—a prerequisite to obtaining the degree. Here a teaching certificate is unnecessary.

Teaching at the university level is done by both graduate students, called teaching assistants or teaching fellows, and professors. The term professor, however, must be clarified. There are three categories of professor in a university: assistant professor, associate professor, and full professor; the last has been granted tenure, the associate is almost always tenured, and the assistant has usually just begun the process. In addition to professors there are lecturers, persons who are not being considered for a tenured post but teach various classes by contractual agreement. Lecturers do not usually have PhDs but have special skills that eminently qualify them to teach their subject. In language instruction, many college and university lecturers are native speakers of the language, sometimes political exiles, emigrés, or writers.

The graduate students teach only undergraduate classes in the area in which they're working for their PhD. They are paid $700 to $1,000 per semester per class they teach out of which they pay tuition for graduate studies. The teaching that graduate students do while working for the PhD is excellent experience for the later teaching they will do as professors. Teaching assistants teaching elementary language courses often find the work invaluable for brushing up on the finer points of grammar and syntax. When you have to explain something to someone else, it has the effect of making it clearer in your own mind.

Teaching at the college and university level is a demanding job, a job that requires intellectual discipline as well as creative thinking. As with all teaching, one has to care about one's students; at this level the thoughts and training that they receive from you can be the most important in their professional and sometimes their personal lives.

Private Schools

Teaching foreign languages in private, commercial language schools is another possibility for the graduate with native-level proficiency in a language.

New York alone has more than fifty commercial language schools. Berlitz, one of the better-known names in language schools, has twenty-nine centers and some sixty schools throughout the United States.

Most of these schools do not have a full-time staff. Their teachers are free-lance, affiliated with the school but not under contract. Schools usually maintain a list of qualified teachers and the hours and days of the week when they are available to teach. If in a given week no students come in who want to learn Russian, the teachers of Russian on the list get no work and no pay. Given the uncertainty surrounding the number of hours that one can work a week, this job must be considered a part-time one. It should be mentioned that the other source of income could be another language school; theoretically one could be registered with a number of schools. The difficulty, however, is that scheduling might prove a nightmare. Because none of your teaching times could overlap, it would be hard to figure out which times to give to which school to ensure the maximum use of your time while fitting in with the schedules of the schools. Many teachers do private tutoring in the times they haven't allocated to a school. That is discussed in the next section.

Salary at private language schools is calculated on an hourly basis and varies from school to school. As mentioned in the introduction, some languages pay better than others, depending on the number of teachers on the market who can teach them. Romance languages such as French, Italian, Spanish, and Portuguese are well represented by teachers, and pay for teaching them is therefore in a lower range than pay for teaching languages such as Chinese, Japanese, and Korean. The going rate for teaching Romance languages, is between $10.00 and $14.00 an hour; for other languages, such as Japanese and Arabic, you earn between $10.00 and $18.00 an hour.

Most commercial language schools require their teachers to have a degree, though in some cases native-level proficiency, regardless of where and how it was obtained, is sufficient.

Classes in these schools are usually very small, from private lessons to classes of three or four students. This is a selling point for the school: the fact that classes are small guarantees the students individual attention and a course and pace of study tailored to their needs. This is also a satisfactory situation for the teacher, who has time to concentrate on a student's problems and help him or her to overcome them.

If you wish a list of Berlitz offices around the country, write to Berlitz, 866 Third Avenue, New York, NY 10022, or check your telephone book for a center near you.

Private Tutoring

Private tutoring of languages is potentially much more profitable than working in a private language school. The reason? There is no middleman between you and the student to take a cut of what the student pays. In major cities, the going rate for private tutoring by a certified professional is between $20.00 and $30.00 an hour.

The major obstacle in teaching privately is finding pupils. Working for a school eliminates that worry, but working for yourself it is the greatest concern. Most private teachers advertise in the personal column of a newspaper. Local papers are best, since your pupils will probably not want to travel hours to see you or vice versa. Another method of advertising is to put your name and telephone number on bulletin boards in schools, at colleges, in cafes, and in supermarkets. You'll be right beside people who want to sell bicycles, get rides to California, or give flute lessons, but that is just what you want. As you develop more and more clients/pupils your reputation will grow, because the best advertising of all is word of mouth.

The advantage of teaching privately is that you are your own boss. You can work as much or as little as you want, at home or in the offices or homes of your pupils. Your schedule can be as flexible as you choose. Often teaching privately is a matter of feast or famine. When you have students, there may be even more who want to come, so many perhaps that you can't accommodate all of them. When you have time to teach you may find that everyone is away on vacation and there are no pupils at all.

Another problem the private tutor faces is scheduled students failing to show up for their hour. In a school you'd be paid whether they showed or not. Teaching privately you can get stuck. That is why it's a good idea to be paid in advance before starting with a pupil. By being paid a week at a time—a month sometimes is even better—you protect yourself against students not showing and later asking to make up the hour. The private tutor must take his job very seriously. He or she must plan the lessons carefully, have materials and teaching aids on hand, and make the most of the time allotted. It is easy to get chatty with your students, especially when many of them come to you directly from work and are tired. You do yourself and them a disservice if you do not push them to learn. Like teaching at a commercial language school, private tutoring is not steady, but when you are busy you can do very nicely.

For more general information on teaching foreign languages, write:

American Council on the Teaching of Foreign Languages
579 Broadway
Hastings-on-Hudson, NY 10706

The Modern Language Association of America
62 Fifth Avenue
New York, NY 10011

Joint National Committee for Languages
300 I Street, NE
Washington, DC 20002

For more information on teaching specific foreign languages, write:

American Association of Teachers of Arabic
1740 Massachusetts Avenue, NW
Washington, DC 20036

American Association of Teachers of Esperanto
4710 Dexter Drive, #9
Santa Barbara, CA 93110

American Association of Teachers of French
57 East Armory
Champaign, IL 61820

American Association of Teachers of German
National Office, Suite 201
523 Building, Route 38
Cherry Hill, NJ 08034

American Association of Teachers of Italian
Edoardo A. Lebàno, President
Department of French and Italian
Indiana University
Bloomington, IN 47405

American Association of Teachers of Slavic and
   European Languages
Joseph Malik, Jr., Executive Secretary-Treasurer
Department of Russian
University of Arizona
Tucson, AZ 85721

American Association of Teachers of Spanish and Portuguese
James R. Chatham, Executive Director
Mississippi State University
Mississippi State, MS 39762-5720

Teaching English as a Foreign Langage

Teaching English as a Foreign Language (TEFL) is a venture that requires charisma, daring, and, of course, fluency in a language. It provides an exciting and challenging way of learning about a country and its people while enabling you to improve your language skills and broaden your knowledge and outlook. If you decide to go overseas, you need not feel alone, though often it is a lone undertaking. According to U.S. Department of State estimates, approximately 1,500,000 nongovernment Americans and their dependents reside in foreign countries, and the total number of U.S. citizens abroad, including nongovernment Americans, civilian U.S. government employees, their dependents, and U.S. military personnel, is well over 2,250,000.

Most foreign schools follow the same school year as in the U.S., from September to June; however, depending on climate, some schools begin in January or May. For information on individual schools see Appendix C, which lists sources. For most teaching positions, including subjects other than TEFL, proficiency in two languages is mandatory. At present, the greatest need exists for high school teachers of English, math, chemistry, biology, and music in Ghana, Hong Kong, India, Japan, Taiwan, and Turkey.

The United States Information Center (USIA, which is discussed further in Chapter V) offers two programs for Teaching English as a Foreign Language.

The Foreign Service English Teaching specialist Program hires on Foreign Service appointment and sponsors teaching programs in the USIA Binational Centers, in autonomous institutions operated by local citizens and American residents and generally independent of the USIA, and in the USIA Information Centers. Because it is a Foreign Service appointment and English Teaching Specialists are expected to administer, lecture, consult, and plan in addition to teaching, applicants must be broad-gauged and experienced: MA/S in Applied Linguistics or a related discipline, academic work beyond the master's degree, and five years' experience Teaching English as a Foreign Language, with some of that time having been abroad. Candidates need not take the Foreign Service exam. You may simply submit Federal application, Standard Form 171 (available from USIA), to English Teaching Specialists, Special Recruitment Section, Room 518, USIA, 301 4th Street, SW, Washington, DC 20547.

The English Teaching Fellow teaches English at a Binational Center for a twelve-month stint. This may be a better way of measuring your interest in TEFL. The Teaching Fellow is not an employee of USIA, although USIA serves as the clearinghouse for applicants. Binational Centers are based primarily in Latin America, with some agencies in Asia, Africa, and Europe. As a Teaching Fellow, you teach on a full-time basis, up to twenty-five hours a week, and you are paid in the currency of the country plus a stipend in dollars. Recent graduates of TEFL and Applied Linguistics may apply; of course, candidates with master's degrees receive special preference. Write to English Teaching Fellow Program, English Teaching Division, at the above address.

If you want to be a bit more independent and daring, you may obtain a list of the 116 Binational Centers and apply directly to one or several of them. In most cases, that means interviewing at the center you have chosen, and unlike the Fellow Program, you must pay your travel expenses. You don't need an academic background in a language, but you must have practical experience. Write the USIA and ask for the list of local names and addresses of the Binational Centers. Before you buy your ticket to Ankara, Turkey, be sure.

The Department of Education offers the Fulbright-Hays Program for teachers of English in other countries on an exchange basis or through placement. You must have a BA and at least three years of teaching experience to qualify. For information and an application, write: Teacher Exchange Section, Office of International Education, U.S. Department of Education, Washington, DC 20202.

If your specialty is Russian and you have experience teaching English as a foreign language, write: USA/USSR, Teacher's Exchange Program, sponsored by AFS International/Intellectual Programs and the Soviet Ministry of Education. The address for AFS International is 313 East 43rd Street, New York, NY 10017.

Other agencies and organizations worth investigating are the Peace Corps (Office of Volunteer Placement, 1990 K Street NW, Washington, DC 20526), the International Schools Service, which recruits teachers for overseas positions (15 Roszel Road, Princeton, NJ 08543), the Modern Language Association, 10 Astor Place, New York, NY 10003), the YMCA (International Division, 356 West 34th Street, New York, NY 10001), and the Office of Personnel and Management (1900 E Street NW, Washington, DC 20415.).

American Schools Overseas

If you don't yet feel ready to teach in a foreign school but still wish to travel and improve your language skills, you can teach in an American school. Proficiency in a language is usually required as well as previous teaching experience. Also, teaching in an American school can prepare you for teaching English in a foreign school, a simple transition once you are already in a country, or for another career later—translating for the United Nations, or serving as a Foreign Service Officer. Time abroad is often a necessity and always a plus when applying for careers using foreign languages.

A good place to apply for a teaching position overseas is through the U.S. Department of Defense. The DOD Dependent Schools accommodate a student population of about 150,000 in 272 schools throughout the world. The school system, established as a consolidated system in 1976, is the eighth largest in the U.S. The Dependent Schools are for the children of DOD military and civilian personnel stationed overseas from kindergarten to twelfth grade. The DOD Dependent School system employs approximately 11,000 people, 9,500 of whom are educators. For lists of schools, write to Overseas Dependent Schools, U.S. Department of Defense, 2461 Eisenhower Avenue, Alexandria, VA 22331. You will receive a list of Army, Navy, and other defense-related stations that have bases in foreign countries and need teachers for their American schools.

Teaching positions at other American schools can be found by writing: Office of Overseas Schools, U.S. Department of State, Room 333, SA-1, Washington, DC 20520; U.S. Department of Education, Division of International Education, 400 Maryland Avenue SW, Washington, DC 20202–5331; and American corporations such as Mobil Oil, Standard Oil, and U.S. Steel, which have established schools for the children of their employees working overseas. *Teach Overseas*, listed in Appendix D, describes colleges, universities, and other schools in 200 countries, giving statistics on the country and its cities, a brief history, and government and professional organizations.

Chapter III

Translation and Interpretation

Outside of teaching, translation and interpretation are the two principal ways of making a career with foreign languages. One may specialize in translation, interpretation, or both.

The two skills are quite different, though related. Translation is the process of rendering the written text of one language into another. Interpretation is verbally rendering the spoken words of one language into another.

The two skills have totally different requirements; hence most people choose one or the other as a specialty. Translators are most concerned with accuracy, whereas interpreters have the additional goal of speed.

Translators work behind the scenes, concerning themselves with treaties, business contracts, specifications, and the like. Interpreters hold center stage; they are in the limelight at conferences, luncheons, and so on, where the participants rely on them to communicate their words to others.

Obviously, interpreters must be accurate in conveying the meaning of one language into another, but because speed is of the essence, they are usually forgiven occasional slips. Translators, on the other hand, cannot afford to make mistakes in their written work. If they have proper working conditions, they have easy access to research material and specialists—in addition to adequate time—to produce an accurate translation that has been checked for error several times. Of course, working conditions are not always ideal, especially when one is working free-lance; tight deadlines and poorly equipped office space would clearly be an impediment, but still the highest standards must be maintained.

What the Jobs Entail

It should be stressed that translation is not merely a process of seeking word-for-word equivalents in the target language for the text in the source language. (The target language is the one translated into; the source language is the one translated from.)

The translator's task is to express in the target language the meaning of what was written in the source language. *Meaning* signifies the sense of a sentence or phrase, a sense that could be complete gobbledegook if a word-for-word translation were used. Language is very much an expression of the culture of a country, one of the major sources of insights into a national mentality—if such a thing exists—into the mores, habits, laws, and taboos of a people. Though similar qualities may be found in peoples speaking different languages, the mere fact that two separate languages have evolved—and bear in mind that languages are constantly evolving—suggests that a unique and exclusive quality exists in a people, as in their language, which is not transferable, which does not find equivalents in other languages.

Let's look at a few common Italian phrases and see how they might be translated into English. Such examples will clearly show the pitfalls that idiom can create in translation. *Non sputare nella minestra che mangi* translates literally into English, "Don't spit into the soup that you eat." Of course, the idiomatic English for that phrase is, "Don't bite the hand that feeds you." Another example is the Italian saying, *L'abito non fa il monaco.* Literally, "The clothing doesn't make the monk." We would, of course, say, "You can't judge a book by its cover."

Interpreters face the same questions in their work, the only difference being that they do not have much time to arrive at a satisfactory resolution of the matter, in fact barely any time at all. Experience is what helps here. The ability to arrive at satisfactory corresponding meanings in two or more languages is the art of translating and interpreting. From what has been said so far, it can be seen that the skill involved is not a purely linguistic one. Both the translator and interpreter must have as broad a cultural base as possible in the languages they deal with. This means a knowledge of literature, art, music, politics, sociology, economics. In fact, one can safely say that translators and interpreters can never know enough and that they must constantly be educating themselves in new areas and becoming more completely versed in already familiar ones. No one suggests that they need be experts in everything—that is patently absurd—but to have a nodding acquaintance with many areas goes a long way in this work.

As we know, each area of human activity has its own specialized vocabulary, words that the nonspecialist would have little occasion to encounter. Translators and interpreters, however, are in an unusual position: they are nonspecialists in the subject in question, yet they must be reasonably familiar with the special or technical terms used in the discussion or text. This means that a prerequisite for being a translator or interpreter is to have a boundless curiosity about many areas in life, a curiosity that seeks its fulfillment in reading and travel and meeting people from different walks of life and from different countries. Translating and interpreting, then, are jobs for the intellectually curious, those for whom a country or a discipline is no limit.

Let's draw a portrait of the type of person who is ideally suited to be a translator, then a portrait of the ideal interpreter. Keep in mind that this is a composite sort of picture, and as such can be either male or female. If you don't think that all your features match all of its features, don't worry.

The ideal translator is a person who can live anywhere in the world and feel comfortable. He travels with a minimum amount of fuss, going to conferences in Geneva one week and in Moscow the next week. He enjoys travel and indeed considers it one of the greatest advantages of the job. He likes to visit new places, taste new foods, meet new people. He immerses himself in the culture of the place where he finds himself, all a part of the self-education process so necessary for his job. He is pleased not to work a nine-to-five day and is perfectly willing to do a night shift, translating documents from an afternoon meeting that must be ready for the morning. He must have a love of words and a sensitivity to them. This love must encompass not only the foreign languages in which he has become accomplished, but also English, so that he can render other languages into suitably clear and potentially elegant English prose. Our ideal translator must be a person who enjoys his own company because he will spend a good deal of time alone, working with texts and dictionaries, newspapers, magazines, files, and reports. He must be self-disciplined: Given a piece to translate by a certain time, he must accomplish the job by that time. Given this, he must be a person able to meet deadlines. These are the personal traits of our translator; let's look now at his qualifications.

There are no ideal qualifications for a translator; each job will require a knowledge of different languages in addition to certain specialized knowledge. For example, one organization might require for a certain conference a translator who knows Russian and French and has some familiarity with nuclear physics. Another conference might need a translator who knows Arabic and is acquainted with oil-drilling techniques. Clearly, a translator cannot be all things to all people, and for this reason he will not be ideally qualified for every position. The question, therefore, becomes what combination of languages and specialized knowledge will make one eminently employable.

The six official languages of the United Nations are Arabic, Chinese, English, French, Russian, and Spanish. To be employed by the United Nations and its agencies, one must be able to translate from at least two official languages into his main language, which itself must be one of the official languages. There are other qualifications needed for employment by the U.N., but they will be discussed later. In the international field of translating, then, knowing two or more of the official U.N. languages is certainly an advantage for the free-lance and a necessity for those who seek full-time employment. That is not to say that these are the only languages in which there is translation work. Italian, Hungarian, or Swahili, to name but three, will also provide occasion for employment. The official languages of the U.N. are, however, the languages in which there is the greatest volume of work to be had.

Let's give our translator a knowledge of French, Russian, and Italian with English as his main language and see how he fares.

What kind of specialized knowledge does he have that is an asset to him on the job? Let's give him a familiarity with international law. He doesn't have a law degree, but he has done enough reading on his own and translated enough legal documents pertaining to international issues that he feels confident and comfortable translating treaties and commercial contracts and in fact has made this his special field of competence.

That brings us to the question of specialization. It is in the interests of every translator to carve out a piece of territory in a particular area where he is especially capable. That well may be in law, medicine, engineering, biology, weaponry; his specialty might be nuclear weapons, chemical engineering, or international law. When one considers the vast amount of technical vocabulary involved in each of these areas, it is clear why such specialization is necessary. The effect of such specialized knowledge on a translator's career cannot be underestimated; he is a rare commodity who possesses a knowledge of Russian, English, and nuclear fission—a desirable translator at any conference concerned with nuclear disarmament.

How can one gain this kind of specialized knowledge? Does one have to go to school and study engineering or law in addition to all the languages that a translator needs? Not necessarily. Most translators gain their specialties through experience. Extended exposure to one subject over the course of many conferences is the first step in the process of familiarizing oneself with a given area. Normally, before a conference begins, the translator is given a full list of related documents so that he can become comfortable with the subject matter. If he finds the material interesting or if he thinks it is material he is likely to come into contact with often, or both, he will begin the process of self-education. He will begin to read up on the subject on his own time, perhaps subscribing to professional journals in an attempt to keep up with the latest events and developments in the field and the new words that inevitably accompany new breakthroughs. Over the years one can build up a reputation as an especially qualified translator in a given area, a reputation that will be constantly reinforced by the new jobs generated from the previous ones.

Just a word here about précis writing. This is a duty that is usually up to the translator to perform. Because it is an integral part of conference translating, its nature should be clearly understood. Précis writing is the process by which the proceedings of a meeting or conference are recorded. Depending on the type of record needed—a full report, called a verbatim record, or a summary of the proceedings, called a summary record—précis writers working usually in teams of three attend conferences and take the notes necessary to render all that occurred into a written record. When verbatim records are necessary, précis writers have access to tapes from the sessions, copies of all speeches, and pertinent documents. Précis writers must have the auditory comprehension skill of the interpreter plus stenographic ability plus expertise in writing.

Great! Our translator has a reputation for being particularly adroit at translations from Russian, French, or Italian into English in the area of international law. Let us say he is not working full time for an international organization—the method for doing so will be discussed later—but is working free-lance. He is in an enviable position in terms of the opportunities open to him. He will probably be able to travel the world working as a free-lance conference translator. The possibility of staying at home and working for law firms that do business with the Soviet Union, Italy, and French-speaking parts of the world is also open. He can make similar agreements with import-export firms dealing with those countries. As a free-lance it's up to him to keep abreast of affairs in his area of specialization and to seek out work based on his knowledge of recent developments. He will also, of course, be registered with a number of translation agencies that act as clearinghouses for translators, providing work but also taking a commission. But more of all that later. Suffice it to say that with the right skills, a translator can do quite well for himself.

What about interpreters? In what way do they have to be different from translators? The main attribute necessary for the interpreter that the translator doesn't need is verbal facility in a number of languages. Whereas the translator can largely rely on passive knowledge of other languages, meaning here the ability to understand but not reproduce a language, the interpreter must rely on active knowledge of a language, which means the ability to speak it. The interpreter must have the same sort of curiosity about life that the translator has. He must like to travel, moving from city to city as conference work demands and doing so with ease. Again like the translator, he must be well versed in a number of subjects and must constantly educate himself in new ones. The more he knows about a lot of things, the more effective he will be in his job.

The character of the interpreter must differ from that of the translator as regards the social side of his nature. The interpreter deals with people, not texts. He must be gregarious, able to handle himself calmly and confidently among people. He can't be inhibited, since ''public speaking'' constitutes a large part of his job. He must be completely fluent in his languages. Idiomatic expressions, slang, even folk sayings must be quickly and competently handled. The interpreter, sitting as he does during a conference in a glass booth with earphones on his head, is on stage. All ears are attuned to his words. All eyes are often upon him. For this reason, it is important that the interpreter convey the meaning of the words he is interpreting with appropriate facial expressions and gestures if need be. It only confuses those watching and listening if the interpreter is relating something funny and yet wears a serious, tense face of concentration or ill humor. An interpreter, therefore, has to be something of an actor as well; his role is the person for whom he is interpreting.

Two methods of interpretation are used, simultaneous and consecutive. In simultaneous interpretation, the interpreter verbally translates what the speaker is saying while he is speaking. In consecutive interpretation, the speaker delivers part or all of the speech, and then the interpreter renders it into the target language. Both types of interpretation require special talents and abilities. Simultaneous interpretation requires lightning fast thinking and complete fluency in the language. Consecutive interpretation requires equal fluency and a superb memory besides.

Interpretation is a high-pressure job. The interpreter is under constant observation; any hesitation or doubt that he manifests may undermine the confidence of his listeners. If you thrive under pressure, like mixing with delegates, diplomats, and professionals, and enjoy the limelight, interpretation might well be the job for you. On the other hand, if you prefer the tranquility of an office, the luxury of working more or less at your own pace, translation would be the more suitable career.

Where to Get Training

Almost all international agencies, translation bureaus, and businesses require that their employees have a college degree in addition to other qualifications. College, then, is the best place to start your training to be a translator or interpreter. Most four-year colleges offer a BA in modern languages. A student who has a natural ability for languages and is a hard worker will come out of such a program well on the way to a successful career in this field. It is essential for the student to study at least two languages, perhaps majoring in one and having the other as a minor, but the more one can handle the better. Some colleges do not allow students to major in a language unless they have studied it in high school; that is something to be checked when applying for various BA programs. The four-year course in a modern language devotes the first two years to the grammar, syntax, and pronunciation of the language as well as developing vocabulary through reading and verbal facility through conversation courses. The second two years are usually spent studying literature in the original language. For example, students of Italian read Dante, Boccaccio, and Petrarch as well as modern authors such as Montale, Calvino, and Moravia. Students of Russian read Pushkin, Chekhov, and Tolstoy as well as modern writers such as Yevtushenko and Solzhenitsyn.

The emphasis on literature in these BA courses is not in itself a bad thing, but for the nascent translator or interpreter these classes only go so far as helping them reach the professional level. Though some classes may be devoted to translations of passages in literary works, this does not provide future translators and interpreters with the breadth of experience that is needed. Only a small portion of all the translation work available involves literary works. As has been stressed throughout this chapter, however, a translator can never know too much; good training in the literature of the language you're studying is excellent for building your passive vocabulary and for learning about the culture of a country. In fact, there are few better insights into a people than those provided by the writings of their great authors. All these factors, in addition to the pure pleasure provided by the study of literature, make extensive reading in a number of languages very helpful for both the translator and interpreter.

Besides the study of literature, the language student will probably also take courses in linguistics, which will prove very helpful in gaining some understanding of the nature of language. Comparative linguistics will provide useful insights into the differences between languages and why these differences exist. Though instruction in these fields is largely theoretical, everything a person knows about the materials of his trade—language for the translator and interpreter—is useful. Indeed, students who are thinking about translating and interpreting as a career would do well to lay as broad a foundation as possible by studying, in addition to languages, subjects in history, art, economics, international relations, and the sciences.

The sciences are sadly neglected by students studying the humanities. This may be regretted later when the translator/interpreter finds himself dealing with technical texts or speeches and has no particular base from which to work and on which to build a specialization. In many colleges, distribution requirements—a certain number of courses that must be taken in a wide range of disciplines before one can graduate—take away from students the temptation to study only the subjects they know they are good at.

Thus far, we have discussed the educational route of earning a BA degree in modern languages with elective courses in a wide range of areas. If the interest and the ability are present, however, the future translator or interpreter can follow another course of study. If you choose to major in a technical or science subject such as engineering or chemistry and also take a language, or preferably two, you have already gone a long way toward establishing an area of specialization as a translator and perhaps even as an interpreter. In the job market, the translator with technical training and experience can probably manage as well with fewer languages as can the translator without technical knowledge who knows more languages.

Given the choice, however, it is generally considered preferable to opt for a liberal arts program during the undergraduate career. Considering the trade-off—early specialization against broader knowledge of lesser depth—it is perhaps better for the student to keep open as many options as possible. Most translators say that technical knowledge can be picked up along the way through reading and on-the-job experience. Summer jobs and part-time work can also provide experience in a number of fields.

Some American colleges and universities offer BA programs for translators and interpreters. Perhaps the best known is at Georgetown University, where an undergraduate program can lead to a Cerificate of Proficiency in Translation in English, French, German, Portuguese, Spanish, and sometimes Italian, or Conference Interpreter.

For information about this program write:

> Georgetown University
> School of Languages and Linguistics
> Division of Interpretation and Translation
> 225 Intercultural Center
> Washington, DC 20057

The Monterey Institute of International Studies offers an MA in language in conjunction with either a degree in International Policy Studies or an MBA. For information about this program write:

> Monterey Institute of International Studies
> Department of Translation and Interpretation
> 425 Van Buren Street
> Monterey, CA 93940
> (in English, French, German, Russian, Japanese, and Spanish)

Certification may be obtained from the following institutions:

> University of Pittsburgh
> Department of French and Italian
> 1328 Cathedral of Learning
> Pittsburgh, PA 15260
> (in French, German, Italian, and Spanish)

Georgia State University
Program for Translation and Interpretation
University Plaza
Atlanta, GA 30303

Marygrove College
Department of Modern Languages
Detroit, MI 48221
(certifies every other year in French, German, and Spanish)

Generally speaking, a BA in modern languages is not sufficient to start work as a translator or interpreter. Specialized postgraduate courses are in order. The following universities offer such courses:

Los Angeles City College
855 North Vermont Avenue
Los Angeles, CA 90029

Arkansas University
Program in Literary Translation
Fayetteville, AR 72701

In Canada:
Bureau du Registraire
Université de Montreal
C.P. 6250, Succersale "A"
Montreal, Quebec H3C 3T5

Other colleges and universities offer courses, if not certificates, in translating and interpreting. When all is said and done, however, there is nothing like experience. In the field of translating and interpreting there is no substitute for it. The more you do, the better you get at it. Certain international agencies have posts for students who want work and training during summer vacations. These organizations are listed in the *Yearbook of International Organizations*, which can be found in any reference library. Having obtained addresses and other information from this source, it is only a matter of writing to the head of the English language section to see if there are any openings. Be sure to mention in your letter the dates when you would be available to start work and when you would have to leave. Your résumé or, as it is called in academic circles, curriculum vitae must be enclosed. This is a useful process to go through even if you are unsuccessful in finding a summer job, as it is the exact same process one goes through when looking for a full-time job in earnest. The heads of the language sections are always on the lookout for qualified people and usually keep a file on a promising applicant for future reference. It is good to be in as many of these files as possible, which is why you should write to as many organizations as you're interested in. The *Yearbook of International Organizations* will be mentioned later when we explore in greater detail how the qualified translator and interpreter look for jobs.

There is also the possibility of finding summer work through your college or university. Local businesses when in need of translation or interpreting service often consult the appropriate language department of a nearby college. Though it is usually the graduate students who receive these positions, you still ought to make your interests known to your department chairman. If you are good enough, you may be surprised at the amount of work that comes your way. Of course, you can always start as a free-lance even as an undergraduate. Put an advertisement in a local newspaper or the college paper, stating the languages you feel qualified to translate from and the subjects. *Be very careful not to take on a project that you can't handle*. Making exaggerated claims about one's abilities does harm to the profession of translating and interpreting as a whole. Standards must be kept high.

Where the Jobs Are

Let's start our survey of jobs in this field by looking at employment by the United Nations and its agencies. As is well known, the headquarters of the United Nations is in New York City. As the forum for international dialogue, the UN has a constant need for translators and interpreters. There are opportunities for qualified people to work either as full-time staff members or free-lance. Here are the qualifications one needs to apply and the method for doing so:

Interpreters—Interpreters are recruited by individual examination. They are required to interpret into their main language, which must be one of the six official languages (Arabic, Chinese, English, French, Russian, and Spanish) and must have a thorough knowledge of three of the languages. Applicants must hold a degree from a university and must have 200 documented days of experience as a conference interpreter. Those who do not meet this requirement but are graduates of interpretation/translation schools may be considered for a Training Programme.

Translator/Précis-writers—Recruitment is by competitive examination and interview. English translator/précis-writer applicants must know French and one other of the six official languages. All other applicants must know English and one other language. In addition, all candidates must be graduates of a university where the language of instruction was their main language and must have a wide general knowledge of the countries where the language is spoken, including some knowledge of international political developments and institutions, law, economics, or scientific or technical subjects. Examinations are held when needed in a number of designated cities, including Geneva, New York, and Vienna. An outline of the written examination, which lasts two days, appears in Appendix E. Residents of Europe should apply to:

> Division du Personnel
> Office des Nations Unies
> Palais des Nations
> 1211 Genève 10, Suisse

In addition, African country nationals interested in applying as a translator/précis-writer for the Economic Commission for Africa in Addis Ababa (Ethiopia) may test for a seven-month training course. Successful trainees go on to work for the Economic Commission for Africa for five years. To apply, write:

Personnel Section
Economic Commission for Africa
P.O. Box 3001
Addis Ababa, Ethiopia

All other applicants for both interpretation and translator/précis-writer should apply to:

Recruitment Programmes Section
Office of Personnel Services
United Nations
New York, NY 10017

There are twenty-nine United Nations agencies located all over the world. A full listing of them is given in Appendix D. These agencies exist to deal with special issues. For example, there is the Food and Agriculture Organization (FAO) in Rome and the International Atomic Energy Agency (IAEA) in Vienna.

The specialized agencies do their own recruitment. If you want to work for one of them, it is necessary to write directly to the recruitment section of the agency. Clearly, here, having the necessary specialty—such as legal knowledge for the International Court of Justice—would be a distinct advantage. Americans who want to work for the United Nations Educational, Scientific and Cultural Organization (UNESCO) in Paris can apply to UNESCO, 7 Palace de Fontenoy 75700, Paris, France. Those interested in working for the World Health Organization (WHO) in Geneva can apply to World Health Organization, 20 Avenue Appia 1211, Geneva 27, Switzerland. Here's a sample letter to give an idea of the form and the type of information that ought to be included:

Chief of English Language Section
General Agreement on Tariffs and Trade
Centre William Rappard
154 Rue de Lausanne
1211 Geneva 21, Switzerland

Dear Sir:

I am interested in applying for a position as a conference translator for your organization. I am a graduate of Yale University with a major in German and French. Enclosed is my résumé.*

Would you please inform me when examinations are to be held and if an interview can be arranged near to that date.

Sincerely yours,

George Diamond

It should be mentioned that the examination given by the UN secretariat in New York is usually recognized as valid by other agencies. If the scheduling of the examination in New York is later than when a position in Rome or Vienna, for example, has to be filled, those organizations abroad will usually arrange for you to take their examination.

The salary at the UN and its agencies depends upon the level one has reached. That level is determined by number of years with the organization. P-2 is the starting level for translators, and P-1 for interpreters. The pay is currently as follows:

For assignment to duty stations in Europe, Canada, Cyprus, Malta, and Turkey (European portion) and in the United States of America:

	Minimum gross	*Maximum gross*
P-1	$22,315/year	$31,098/year
P-2	$29,815/year	$40,868/year
P-3	$37,613/year	$53,997/year
P-4	$47,315/year	$65,151/year
P-5	$60,816/year	$76,266/year

P-3 is the level one reaches after two years. For interpreters, P-2 is reached after three to nine months. American citizens, unlike the nationals of a number of other countries working for the UN, are not exempt from taxation. Americans working abroad in a UN agency are subject to the same Internal Revenue code as any other American working abroad.

---

*For sample résumé, see Appendix B.

Working on a free-lance basis for the UN or its agencies presents a slightly different picture both in the application process and the salary scale than that of the full-time staff member. Free-lance translators and interpreters are called short-term staff in UN parlance. They are usually hired to fill a vacancy that cannot be filled from the ranks of the full-time staff. The first step to getting connected with the UN as a free-lance is to take the UN examination and have an interview. If you pass the examination and appear suitable after the interview, you merely state that you are interested in working on a short-term basis and specify when you are available. The various language sections—in the case of Americans it would of course be the English language section—maintain lists of available translators and interpreters. Separate lists are maintained by the translating section and the interpreting section. These departments also have lists from international translating and interpreting associations. Professionally it is exceedingly important to have membership in these organizations, as their lists of accredited members—usually arranged by language capabilities and special subject areas—provide translators and interpreters not only to the UN but also to many businesses, publishers, and international organizations. Here are the names and addresses of five of the most important associations:

American Association of Language Specialists
Suite 9
1000 Connecticut Avenue, NW
Washington, DC 20036

International Association of Conference Interpreters
14 Rue du L'Ancien-Port
CH 1201, Geneva
Switzerland

International Association of Conference Translators
15, route des Morillons
CH-1218 Geneva
Switzerland

International Federation of Translators
Heiveldstraat 245
B-9110 Ghent/St. Amandsberg
Belgium

American Translators Association
109 Croton Avenue
Ossining, NY 10562

In addition, there is the American Translators Association, 109 Croton Avenue, Ossining, NY 10562. Their professional service directory is not utilized by the UN and its agencies but nonetheless provides the free lance with excellent exposure.

One qualifies as a short-term staff member if one's contract with the UN is for a period not exceeding six consecutive months. Pay is on a daily or monthly basis, and the rate varies according to experience. The range is usually $160.50 to $259.50 daily. In addition to the per diem pay there is a daily subsistence allowance, which varies from duty station to duty station. For instance, the current daily subsistence allowance for someone coming from outside the metropolitan area to work in New York is $138. There would be another rate for Geneva and still another for Bangkok. A free lance should get on as many of the lists of the UN agencies as possible. This can be achieved by writing to the Chief of the English Language Section of each agency, enclosing a detailed résumé and a letter giving dates of availability and specialization. If a job should come up, round-trip airfare to the conference city is of course provided. All the contractual agreements, as well as the necessary travel documents, should be arranged before you leave. Indeed, it would be extremely foolish not to take care of these matters well beforehand.

In addition to work either full or part time for the UN or one of its agencies, there are numerous other job possibilities for the qualified translator and interpreter. The *Yearbook of International Organizations*, mentioned earlier in this chapter and available in the reference section of all major libraries, furnishes a list of all international organizations, their addresses, and the times of their conferences. Write to these organizations expressing your interest. Some of them maintain a small staff of permanent translators. At the time of their conferences, they require many more. The number of organizations is indeed so great that potentially one could be kept busy for a good part of the year flying from conference to conference.

Membership in a number of translating and interpreting associations will also provide work. Since many organizations, businesses, and individuals from time to time need translation and interpreting work done, they often call an association and ask for someone qualified. If you are on the list of available people, work is bound to come your way. These associations do not usually determine rates, merely providing a service for their members and the community. Therefore it is up to each individual translator and interpreter to determine his pay scale. Here are some guidelines.

Translators usually charge by the word. Rates vary widely depending on the language and the nature of the material. The American Translation Association offers the following rates per 1,000 words:

	Major European Languages	*Unusual Languages*
Nontechnical	$85.00	$115.00
Semitechnical	90.00	120.00
Technical	95.00	125.00

A competent translator, again depending on the difficulty of the material, should be about to produce about 3,000 words per day. Some manage about 4,000. It should be noted, however, that a text of particular difficulty might slow a translator down to 1,000 words per day.

Interpreters work according to varying rates, depending on the language, where it is simultaneous or consecutive interpreting, and whether it is a large conference, a small business meeting, or one to one. An interpreter of Romance languages could probably expect to earn from $12 to $20 an hour, depending on the nature of the job. For languages such as Japanese or Hungarian the rate usually goes up to $25 to $50 an hour. If the subject matter is particularly technical, the rate goes up yet again. Most interpreters set a two- to three-hour minimum on any job.

According to the American Association of Language Specialists, most professional interpreters at present charge by the day instead of by the hour. It is best to negotiate beforehand the rate that you will charge.

There are numerous commercial translating and interpreting agencies throughout New York City and in most major cities in the United States. It is unusual for such agencies to have a full-time staff of translators and interpreters. They usually maintain a list of available free-lance people with whom they work out schedules as need demands. Translators and interpreters working for these agencies are usually paid according to the rates mentioned above. Looking for a job with one of these agencies is more or less the same process as applying for any job. One could try to set up an appointment for an interview and examination by phone or write a letter of inquiry enclosing one's résumé.

The professions of translating and interpreting figure prominently in many areas of activity. Legal, commercial, medical, scientific, and financial translating and interpreting are needed by individuals, institutions, and businesses in fields that deal with greater or lesser frequency on an international level. Translators and to a lesser extent interpreters can often find full-time employment with businesses and institutions. This will be discussed in the ensuing chapters as we look at various fields and the application of foreign language skills to them.

Escort/Interpreter

The State Department maintains a list of over 1,000 free-lance escort/interpreters. To qualify, you should speak one of the twenty-four languages ranging from Bulgarian and Icelandic to Thai and Spanish. Occasionally, English-speaking escorts are needed for dignitaries from English-speaking countries. Escorts interpret for foreign leaders and technicians and travel throughout the U.S. An assignment usually lasts about 30 days, and the pay is approximately $90 a day with all expenses paid. It is an exciting way to meet dignitaries on a formal and informal basis and to see the country.

For information, write to U.S. Department of State, Language Services Division, Washington, DC 20520. An outline of the test is given in Appendix E.

Conclusion

The field of translating and interpreting can offer an exciting and varied way of life. Through it is not a field where one can become a millionaire, it is one that provides for stimulating work, constant education, and the opportunity to meet and work with interesting people and to travel. Students interested in communication, fascinated by other cultures, or curious about different fields of learning will probably be happy as either a translator or an interpreter.

Whether one decides to work for the UN or one of its agencies, for business, government, or as a free-lance will largely set the tenor of one's work. Some assignments will prove more agreeable than others, but as a professional all must be handled with the scrupulous care that must be maintained as the hallmark of the profession.

Experience is the best teacher in the field of translating and interpreting. A college degree and a master's in translating are both important qualifications; nonetheless, practical experience in the workplace is what will give you the confidence and expertise necessary to handle different types of assignments well and with aplomb.

Translating and interpreting is the most direct application of one's knowledge of a foreign language to the working world. In this field, linguistic ability must be mixed with a wide-ranging knowledge of world affairs and other areas to allow those practicing this art to function as mediums of expression for parties who would otherwise be unable to communicate.

Chapter IV

Business and Finance

The worlds of business and finance are nothing if not international. In U.S. business, thinking and acting internationally is an economic necessity. The country needs foreign markets. We produce so much that it cannot all be absorbed domestically. This dependence on foreign trade makes us the largest trading nation in the world.

American companies are always looking to expand their markets. Because of the restrictive import laws of some countries, it has often been necessary for American companies to establish branch offices and even manufacturing plants in the host country in order to exploit that country's market. This has sometimes necessitated going into partnership either with a company in the host country or with the government itself. The reason various countries insist on this practice is to provide new employment opportunities for their people.

A number of American companies are literally worldwide. We need only think of giants like Exxon, IBM, Ford, and General Electric to realize how some American companies have succeeded in establishing themselves from Moscow to Rio de Janeiro. There are also companies that have branch offices and representatives in one or two foreign countries, operating much like the giants but on a smaller scale. Recent statistics show that over 3,200 U.S. corporations with over 22,500 subsidiaries and affiliates are operating abroad.

In dollar volume the United States imports more than it exports. We are dependent on various countries for numerous raw materials: coffee, tea, sugar, exotic metals, and, of course, oil. In order to contract for such materials, it is necessary for many companies to have a large staff of buyers whose job it is to go abroad and secure those materials.

Raw materials are not the only things we import. Consider the vast number of Japanese television sets, computers, and automobiles on the U.S. market. Look in the department stores and see the prevalence of French clothes, Italian shoes. The latest statistics available indicate that more than 2,700 foreign firms have branches and representatives in the United States.

What does all of this mean for the student who is looking for a career involving foreign languages? It means that the tremendous amount of world trade generates jobs in which a knowledge of a foreign language is a definite asset. Here we are speaking about language skills in addition to management, technical, clerical, or financial skills. The need for translators in these companies is also great.

Management

College graduates with degrees in business, economics, and liberal arts areas such as history or English will find that they are well prepared for management positions in business. Needless to say, one is much better qualified with an MBA degree (Master of Business Administration). All other things being equal in educational background, an applicant with knowledge of one or more foreign languages will have a distinct advantage. Given the old American arrogance toward the learning of other languages, the corporate mentality with its tunnel vision, and the rise of the technocrat, there has been a dearth of qualified executives and managers with a knowledge of other languages and cultures. Such people are now in demand.

The following is a list of some of the outstanding companies that employ people with both language and business skills:

Exxon Corp.   Shell Oil
General Motors   The Stanley Works

Ford

Texaco

Mobil

Standard Oil of California

Gulf Oil

IBM

General Electric

Chrysler

International Tel & Tel

Navistar

Coca-Cola Co.

Du Pont

Litton Industries

American Express

Procter & Gamble

Tenneco

Union Carbide

Westinghouse Electric

Goodyear Tire & Rubber

Phillips Petroleum

As American business expands into foreign markets and foreign firms seek to sell the American market, the executive comfortable in another language should not be surprised to find that his linguistic fluency translates into increased sales, better business relations, and greater ease in day-to-day business. Here's what the personnel director of a large cosmetics manufacturer said at their New York headquarters:

We're often on the lookout for new people to fill various management positions that open up, or as our market expands, are newly created. We need marketing managers, production managers, advertising managers, and financial officers who are able to think and operate in terms greater than our domestic sales. Some of the jobs available are in fact overseas. We need to fill these posts with people who have a knowledge of the language and country in question. Just consider the area of advertising. Ads that are effective in the United States might prove disastrous in another country where they might offend national or religious sensibilities. Our advertising staff must be aware of these issues and must be sufficiently capable in another language to coordinate efforts to get the right message across, to project the right image. We recently ran a want ad in the New York *Times* announcing a position available for a production manager with at least three years in the business who spoke and wrote Japanese fluently. We wanted to send this person to our

Tokyo office to run the production and packaging department there. The salary of the job was $30,000 plus a cost
of living adjustment for the high cost of living in Tokyo.
We had ten applicants and the man we finally chose is still
there.

From those remarks we are able to gain some insight into the
kinds of opportunities available in one particular firm. It should be
noted that the $30,000 salary mentioned is not an average salary.
Experience and particular language skills fitted together to fill a
need. Generally speaking, the salary range for a management-level
job in which fluency in a language or languages is required is between
$20,000 and $68,000 a year.

A woman who started an import-export firm ten years ago told us
in an interview that her knowledge of Spanish literally started her in
business. Here's what she had to say:

When I was a student I majored in Spanish. I was fascinated
by South American literature and made a number of trips
to Peru, Argentia, and Bolivia. It was when I was down
there that I came across the most beautiful handicrafts, bas-
kets, blankets, wooden sculpture. I started bringing these
things back to the States for friends as presents. Everyone
who received one of these gifts loved them and other friends
would always comment on them. Just before I was about to
graduate from college I made what I thought might be my
last trip to Peru for a while. Over the years I had made some
friends so I wanted to say goodbye. One of my friends in
Lima had a handicraft shop that had been in his family for
generations. it was over dinner one night that we got this
great idea to import these goods to the States where I would
distribute them, and from the States I would export to him
American sweaishirts and T-shirts. I haven't looked back

since; business took off the first year and I have enlarged my organization four times in as many years. I now do business not only with Peru but also with Bolivia and Venezuela. Three years ago I started studying Portuguese. I wanted to open up the Brazilian market and there were numerous items I was interested in handling here that I saw there on my first trip five years ago. If you're interested in knowing the correlation between languages and business, all I can tell you is that since I've felt fairly fluent in Portuguese my business in Brazil rose from nothing to $1.5 million yearly. I'm not saying that just being able to speak Portuguese allowed me to make this kind of money. Obviously, my experience over the years has given me a lot of business know-how. What I am saying is that my familiarity with the market, the people, and the culture has allowed me to deal with an ease and confidence that is definitely an advantage to my business. Quite frankly, I don't think I could be nearly so effective if I had to rely on translators and interpreters to help me conduct my affairs. A lot of my business is based on my personal relationships with suppliers in South America; I've made thousands of dollars worth of deals on a handshake. One simply can't establish this sort of trust through an interpreter. Because of my ability to communicate in their language, I'm not considered an ugly American trying to exploit them. We have a mutual trust, and this trust emanates in large part from our ability to communicate with ease.

Not everyone will be as fortunate as this woman in finding a business future as a direct result of language study. It is interesting to note, however, how much importance was attributed to speaking Spanish and Portuguese in establishing trust, friendship, and ultimately credibility with those she dealt with.

Though there is no denying that English is the language of international business, the advantages accruing through ability to conduct and conclude business in the language of one's opposite number are so great, not only in real profit but also in more intangible feelings of goodwill, that executives cannot afford to ignore them.

Clerical and Secretarial Work

One area that provides possibly the greatest opportunities for employment in the business sector, as well as being among the easiest to enter, is clerical and secretarial work that requires knowledge of other languages. Many executives do not have the language skills necessary to do their job most effectively. If a corporation does much business abroad, if there are overseas branches to be supervised, if clients from abroad visit the U.S., an executive without language skills must have someone to help deal with the correspondence, business lunches, and reports that are generated as a result of being an international concern. The person who can fulfill this function admirably is the secretary or administrative assistant who is bilingual or more.

Language skill alone is usually not sufficient for getting a job as a bilingual secretary. Applicants must have secretarial skills including typing and perhaps word processing—fifty to sixty words a minute is about average, shorthand in English and sometimes in the foreign language, bookkeeping, correspondence. Regarding the ability in another language, fluency is optimal but not always required. Reading and translating correspondence, writing and typing answers in the foreign language, arranging meetings, and sorting out difficulties by telephone in the other language are all duties that a bilingual secretary will be called upon to do. Knowledge of the field itself is also very important. Secretaries should be familiar with, or at least familiarize themselves with, the workings of the industry and the terms and specialized vocabulary, both in English and the foreign language, necessary in conducting business.

Ads for jobs for bilingual secretaries often appear in the help-wanted section of the newspapers of most major cities. A sample survey suggests that French, German, and Spanish are the languages most in demand, but Portuguese, Japanese, and Italian are often listed as well. Jobs as bilingual secretary and administrative assistant are available in such diverse fields as public relations, architecture, international banking, law, import-export, publishing, film, textiles, public affairs, fashion, and international brokerage. Salaries for these jobs range between $15,000 and $35,000 per annum.

On the facing page is a clipping from an issue of the New York *Times* Sunday employment section.

As can be seen from these advertisements, many of the jobs are to be obtained through agencies. Upon inquiry an interview will be arranged to determine your suitability and potential. If the job you are applying for is already filled or for one reason or another denied you, these agencies will keep you on their lists and try to help you find a position. Usually the agency fee is paid by the employer, not the applicant. In looking at the salaries advertised, you will sometimes see the letter K, for example, "sec/asst to Dir. $24K." K means $1,000.

Generally speaking, a person with language and secretarial skills will make more money than one with only secretarial skills. More important, perhaps, the job is usually more interesting in that more responsibility and creative freedom are given to the bilingual secretary than the one who is not. An executive will rely more and more on a secretary who shows through good work that he or she is able to handle greater responsibility; this state of affairs is increased when the executive must also rely on the secretary for language skills.

Being a bilingual secretary is an excellent way to get a foot in the door of an industry that might otherwise be difficult to enter. This is why many administrative assistant and secretarial jobs are called entry-level positions. Once inside the organization, there are usually many opportunities for a advancement. Ability in a number of other languages certainly increases one's prospects. This is especially true with companies that are expanding and opening offices abroad. A number of people who started as bilingual secretaries and gained experience in the workings of the firm and the industry have advanced to managerial positions in the country where their foreign language was spoken.

Technical Expertise

Language ability in engineers and other personnel is of great importance in companies producing machinery or involved in construction, mining, or chemical production when the companies set up plants overseas or work under contract for foreign firms or governments. In addition to American companies working overseas, foreign-based companies have set up subsidiaries in the United States and need skilled technical people who can function in the language of the parent company.

Consider a manufacturer of machinery that is produced in the United States but exported to Europe. Such a company needs engineers familiar with the various components and general functioning of the equipment and able to write detailed instructions and specifications concerning the equipment in the language of the country that is the target market. Alternatively, components imported to the United States and assembled here may not have specifications in English. If the components come from several countries, the task of putting everything together utilizing the diagrams and descriptions in two or three languages is a large one. Technicians and engineers with language ability are often the only people equal to the task. Given the technical nature of the material, a professional translator would probably not be up to it; far better the technical man with a knowledge of the languages in question.

Construction companies building overseas—in some cases constructing entire cities where desert had been before—find that engineers who can deal with technical questions in the language of the country greatly facilitate any project, saving time, money, and aggravation in being able to ascertain what is wanted and coordinate it with what is needed.

It must be stressed that knowledge of a foreign language alone is not enough to be hired in these very technical areas. Degrees in engineering or draftmanship, or training as a technician in addition to some years of experience are usually prerequisites for the kinds of jobs we've been discussing. Language skills are an asset. Combined with the appropriate technical knowledge, they can make a person a very valuable and relatively rare commodity on the job market.

Banking and Finance

International banking and finance is a necessary adjunct of international business. As companies expand into foreign markets, banking facilities must be established abroad to deal with the new flow of business. Whereas local correspondent banks were once considered adequate means of service for any company that did business in faraway places, American banks now see their presence in these places as advantageous both to them and their customers as the volume of international trade increases. The whole range of banking services—letters of credit, loans, clearance of checks, transfer of money, conversion of currencies—is handled on a worldwide scale by banks that have established themselves all over the world. Just as American banks have opened offices abroad, so have foreign banks opened in the United States. Business has taken advantage of expanded markets; now, so have the banks.

With the increased scale of international banking, the need for qualified multilingual staff is also considerable. Accountants, clerks, bank officers, auditors, credit analysts, commercial and personal loan officers, administrative assistants to top administrators with knowledge of foreign languages will find opportunities both in the United States and abroad.

Working for an American bank in the United States, the need to know a foreign language might arise in dealing with a branch in a community where English is not the language most people speak. A Spanish-speaking loan officer, for example, would be invaluable in a Spanish-speaking neighborhood. Besides making his job easier, the officer increases the usefulness of the bank in the community as well as the amount of business the bank does. Working for an American bank in the U.S. but in the international division requires the banking officer to be familiar with the language and culture of the country or countries to which he or she is assigned as well as the financial and political issues crucial in day-to-day transactions.

Clearly, the world of finance cannot be divorced from any other aspect of the world.

In working for a foreign bank in the United States, the need for familiarity with the language and banking practices of another country becomes even more apparent. Since one's immediate superior may well be a national of the country where the bank has its home office, and since a large part of the business one transacts will involve a company or residents of that country, it is essential for the proper exercise of one's duties as well as effective public relations that one be comfortable and competent in the language in question.

American banks with branches abroad need multilingual staff in almost all divisions. Though much of the staff will be nationals of the host country, top administrative and supervisory positions usually are filled by Americans. The necessity of being able to communicate well with both personnel and customers makes knowledge of a foreign language a real priority. Most banks seeking employees to fill these positions look for people with either training or experience in financial analysis and familiarity with the country in question either through study or extended periods of residence or both. Bankers are aware that personnel must be capable in handling not only money but people; speaking the language of a customer can be essential.

On the facing page is a sample of jobs advertised in the classified section of the New York Sunday *Times*:

To gain a further idea of the scope of banking jobs using foreign languages, let's look at Chase Manhattan, the third largest bank in the United States. Currently Chase Manhattan Bank receives about 50,000 foreign-language communications a month. A multilingual staff deals with this vast flood of paper. French, German, Spanish, Italian, and Portuguese are the five working languages. In addition, the bank's translation division can handle Russian, Hungarian, Czech, Hebrew, and Estonian. Chase Manhattan has twenty-nine overseas offices and deals with 51,000 correspondent banks all over the world. All executive officers of the bank need to be proficient in at least one foreign language.

It should be remembered in reference to the field of banking and finance, as with all the other areas mentioned in this chapter, that language skill alone is not sufficient to secure a position. Jobs in banking usually require the applicant to have a degree in business, economics, or mathematics. A degree in the humanities is also feasible if one shows an aptitude for math. An MBA is, of course, one of the greatest assets one can have. Most banks run their own training program, the successful completion of which is the first step to a career. Students desiring more information about these training programs can write to the personnel office of the bank that interests them.

Before ending this discussion of banking and finance, mention should be made of a career with the International Bank for Reconstruction and Development, or the World Bank. The World Bank is an international organization dedicated to providing financial assistance for economic development. With its two affiliates, the International Development Association (IDA) and the International Finance Corporation (IFC), the World Bank operates throughout the world as a specialized agency of the United Nations. A booklet on careers with the World Bank defines the organization as:

. . . a banking institution, guided by sound principles of banking in its lending operations. It is, at the same time, a development institution. Besides lending funds, it provides technical assistance to its borrowers in a wide range of areas, from the merely technical to broad development policies, planning, organization, and management. A service especially appreciated by borrowers is the Bank's assistance in the identification, preparation, and the implementation of projects.

Clearly, for a student interested in an international banking career where the knowledge of languages is a tremendous asset, where broad cultural knowledge and wide economic perspective are appreciated, the World Bank is an organization worth considering. The World Bank has thirty-five offices around the world. Although 95 percent of the staff remains in the headquarters in Washington, D.C., they are expected to travel. There is a wide range of jobs within the organization, the backbone of the professional staff being composed of loan officers, economists, and specialists.

Candidates for employment are recruited from all the member nations. The selection process is competitive. The Bank is looking for young university graduates who, through a sense of public service and a desire to be effective through the utilization of their abilities, want to make a career with the World Bank.

For more information students should write to:

Personnel Department
World Bank
1818 H Street NW
Washington, DC 20433

Chapter V

Careers in Government

Government in the United States is staffed by civil servants. The Federal government is the largest single employer in the country, and state and local government provides employment for workers in innumerable capacities.

Knowledge of a foreign language is a prerequisite for certain jobs in government. In others being bilingual or multilingual is a definite advantage and in some cases means higher pay.

Relatively few translators and interpreters are employed as such by government. The State Department has a staff of only fifty. Most bilingual servants use their language skills in connection with their other areas of professional expertise. Among people in this category are foreign service officers stationed in American embassies and consulates around the world, immigration inspectors, police officers, and social workers.

As the largest single employer, the Federal government also employs the greatest number of people who possess language skills. Three agencies that particularly need qualified people with a knowledge of languages are the Department of State, the United States Information Agency, and the Agency for International Development. In some instances these agencies have been less effective than they might have been because of not having staff with the appropriate language skills to handle specific situations, sometimes emergencies. An example is the case a few years ago in Kabul, Afghanistan, when a Russian soldier defected and sought asylum in the American embassy and there was not one Russian-speaking staff member to interview him. A concerted effort is being made by many U.S. agencies to fill language gaps.

Employees of local government, responding to the needs of various ethnic communities, often feel duty-bound to learn the language of the people they are dealing with. Social workers in Hispanic neighborhoods find that they cannot do their job effectively without Spanish. Many of these social service jobs require that candidates be bilingual in Spanish. Police officers in New York City face the same problem when working in Hispanic neighborhoods and are encouraged to attend Spanish language classes provided by the police department. In recruitment, knowledge of Spanish is considered a definite asset.

The Foreign Service

The Foreign Service of the United States is America's diplomatic, consular, commercial, and overseas cultural and information service. Foreign Service Officers serve under the Departments of State and Commerce. Foreign Service Specialists are officers with special expertise that assists the Foreign Service in the performance of its duties. Among them are doctors and nurses, communications specialists, financial managers, secretaries, and members of many other professions as well. Foreign Service personnel must represent America abroad, supporting American policy publicly whatever their private views may be. They act in administrative, consular, economic, commercial, and political capacities both in the Department of State in Washington and in 230 U.S. embassies and consulates around the world. Foreign Service Information Officers are members of the United States Information Agency and act as public affairs, information, and cultural officers in USIA headquarters in Washington, in other government agencies, and in embassies and consulates abroad.

A job with the Foreign Service means that 60 percent of one's career will be spent abroad, transferring from post to post every two to four years. It is an exciting profession, one in which international affairs are a day-to-day concern.

The specific duties of the Foreign Service vary from department to department. Generally speaking, the task of the whole service is to maintain relations with other nations; that is, to act as the diplomatic channel through which American policies, interests, and wishes can be expressed. As America's representative abroad, the service is also able to keep a finger on the pulse of the host country, to make on-the-spot evaluations of political and economic developments that have both domestic and international repercussions.

Among the positions filled by Foreign Service Officers are administrative officers supervising budget and fiscal planning, general services, personnel, security, and communications; consular officers working with the public and dealing with visa issuance, passports, and many other issues that relate directly to both foreigners and American nationals abroad; political affairs officers analyzing and reporting on political issues and communicating American foreign policy to the government of the country in which they are stationed; economic officers in Washington working with money matters, investment, and economic trends affecting U.S. interests. To encourage and help U.S. export and investment abroad, a new division of the Foreign Service, the Foreign Commercial Service, came into being in 1980. Commercial Officers act as liaison between American and foreign business, promoting U.S. trade, and assisting when necessary to resolve trade or investment disputes. Working for the United States Information Agency are Foreign Service Information Officers (FSIO). These officers are perhaps the members of the Foreign Service most responsible for "public diplomacy"; that is, helping the peoples of other nations understand U.S. policies and thinking, assisting in the dissemination of information to other nations, and making the cultures of other countries more accessible to Americans. The FSIO abroad may be the press attaché, holding press conferences and briefings for the media to explain new developments in U.S. policy. The FSIO may be the cultural affairs officer or cultural attaché, arranging educational and cultural exchanges, lectures, concerts, and athletic events both at home and abroad in an attempt to encourage international understanding. An FSIO usually spends six to ten years abroad before returning for a two- to three-year stint in

Washington, D.C. In Washington the FSIO is involved in coordination of the agency's activities abroad, often being responsible for film production, periodical publication, and video enterprises. The FSIO is sometimes assigned to the Voice of America, the United States' broadcasting service, which we shall discuss in the next chapter.

If these types of jobs appeal to you, if the prospect of spending the majority of your professional life abroad is attractive, if the idea of representing your country and your country's interests is exhilarating, you may well want to consider the Foreign Service as a career. It is certainly a life in which knowledge of a foreign language is a necessity. The Foreign Service Officer must have a wide knowledge of American and world affairs as well as the capability to pursue the study of one area in depth. Most Foreign Service Officers have degrees in a wide variety of subjects.

Selection for the Foreign Service is based on a written examination held the first Saturday in December throughout the country and abroad. Out of the 15,000 people who take the examination, only 250 are chosen to serve. This selection is not based solely on successful completion of the examination, but also on a one-day evaluation during which the candidate is judged by a panel of Foreign Service examiners through interviews and a battery of simulation techniques. Applicants who want to take the test must be at least twenty years of age, U.S. citizens, and available for worldwide assignment.

Salaries depend on one's rank as determined by years of experience and merit. New Junior Officers are given jobs at FSC 6, 5, or 4. This means a salary ranging between $19,460 (FSC-6 minimum) and $39,451 (FSC-4 maximum). Those who enter at the mid-level have an FSC 3, 2, or 1 depending on experience, age, and qualifications. This means a salary between $33,154 (FSC-3 minimum) and $65,642 (FSC-1 maximum). Appointment to Class 1, the Senior Foreign Service Officer position, is very rare.

Clearly, knowledge of a foreign language or languages is a tremendous asset for a Foreign Service job. Consular Officers, for example, can expect to use their language skills daily as they meet with local officials in law enforcement and immigration, foreign nationals, and foreign national employees working in the embassy or consulate.

Here is the policy of the Foreign Service in regard to languages as given in the U.S. Department of State publication 9202 on Foreign Service Careers:

Knowledge of foreign languages is not required for appointment, but once hired, all new officers must demonstrate professional competency in at least one foreign language before the end of their initial probationary period. If necessary, an officer attends classes at the Foreign Service Institute, which offers training in over forty languages. Those who enter with language abilities are tested within thirty days of appointment and, if found proficient in certain designated languages, may receive a higher salary. The Department of State and the USIA particularly seek persons with knowledge of ''hard'' or ''exotic'' languages (e.g., Arabic, Chinese, Russian). Candidates without prior foreign language ability are appointed as language probationers, and they must acquire acceptable language competency before tenure can be granted.

If you wish to obtain more information about the Foreign Service, USIA, and the State Department, write:

Recruitment Division
U.S. Department of State
Box 9317, Rosslyn Station
Arlington, VA 22209

Employment Branch
USIA
301 4th Street, SW
Washington, DC 20547

The State Department's intern programs are for a paid summer or an unpaid quarter or semester during the school year. For more information, write to the Intern Coordinator at the State Department address and ask for the pamphlet "Student Intern Programs" (State Department Publication 9362) and the Standard Form 171.

Also, the Presidential Management Office offers a student internship program for people interested in management and public policy. Write to the State Department for information.

Agency for International Development (AID)

The Agency for International Development is a part of the International Development Agency. The AID was established by Congress in 1961 for the purpose of providing aid in the areas of agriculture, education, finance, engineering, industrial development, health, and population planning to developing countries in Africa, Asia, Latin America, and the Middle East. The assistance programs of the AID exist to help the people of various countries obtain increased productive capacities, improve the quality of life, and encourage economic stability.

The Agency provides a two-year intern program, which was developed in 1968 as a means to train qualified applicants for the specialized AID positions. In 1985 the program was temporarily cancelled for financial reasons; however, the agency keeps applications on file for when classes resume. Their record shows great success. The first class had five applicants who completed their two-year training in 1970. By September 1984, 672 interns had enrolled in 27 classes, and about 75 percent of those who interned with IDI have stayed with AID. Here's how the AID pamphlet defines some minimum requirements for an internship position:

A graduate degree in agriculture, agricultural economics, economics, housing/urban development, international relations, population planning, public health/nutrition, public and business administration, or other closely related disciplines; two or more years of experience; worldwide availability. Maturity, good character, tolerance, sensitivity, and adaptability are essential characteristics for working with host country officials, foreign nationals, and private and voluntary organizations also participating in development projects overseas.

Candidates must be U.S. citizens and a good health. Selection is determined by a competitive process, evaluation of past academic record and experience being in most cases decisive.

Interns serve for twenty-four months, spending eight weeks in group training, one to three months but possibly a year in individual, specialized job training in Washington, D.C., and the remaining time posted abroad.

Interns can be trained in a number of specialties: the area chosen of course is largely based on prior experience. Here are some of the jobs available: *Economist*—analyzes economies of host governments as a basis for economic and technical assistance programs; *Program Officer*—advises Mission Director and staff on AID policy; *Accounting Officer*—keeps financial records according to accounting practices and advises on implications of new transactions; *Housing/Urban Development Officer*—assists in identifying urban problems and advises on programs; *Health/Nutrition/Population Officer*—assists and advises on all health and nutritional programs and problems and advises on population control and family planning; *Administration Management Officer*; *Contract/Commodity Officer*—supervises the getting and shipping of commodities for AID projects and administers contracts, grants, and other agreements between host countries and institutions; *Education/Human Resources Development Officer*—develops educational systems for host countries; *Project Development Officer*—helps with implementation of AID projects and monitors projects; *Agricultural-Rural Development Natural Resources Officer*—assists host government in managing natural resources and advises on economics involving food production.

All of these jobs require special skills that can usually be gained only in specific courses of study. Although language ability alone is not sufficient to qualify one for a job with the AID, it is not a skill that an AID officer can be without. Here is what the AID pamphlet has to say on foreign languages:

Foreign language proficiency is required for tenure in the Foreign Service. IDIs must have foreign language proficiency or they will receive training after employment. Preferred languages are French, Spanish, and certain other languages such as Arabic, spoken in the developing countries.

Beginning salaries with the AID are between $22,000 and $45,000, depending on qualifications.

Students wishing to obtain further information should write:

International Development Intern Program
Recruitment Division, PM-RS
2401 E Street
Room 1430
Washington, DC 20523

Federal Bureau of Investigation

The FBI is an organization surroundedly by a certain aura of glamour, perhaps because of the many books, films, and television programs that have taken their theme from its activities. What exactly does the FBI do? The FBI is a law-enforcement agency that investigates violations of the laws of the United States; crimes such as kidnapping, extortion, bank robbery, and espionage fall within its province. At present, the FBI employs close to 8,000 Special Agents assigned to its 59 field offices throughout the U.S.

The investigative work is conducted by the Special Agents. To qualify to be an agent one must be a graduate of a state-accredited law school with at least two years of resident undergraduate work; a graduate of a four-year resident college with a major in accounting or another economic field of study with a Public-Acountant Certificate; a graduate of a four-year accredited college with fluency in a foreign language(s) currently in demand by the FBI; a graduate of a four-year accredited college with three years' full-time work experience;

or a PhD, an MA or a BA graduate in electrical engineering or metallurgy, or an MA or a PhD in other science and computer related fields. Applicants must be at least twenty-three years of age and no older than thirty-five. In addition, there are desired weight requirements and a physical fitness test.

The salary grade for entering Special Agents is GS-10, paying $26,261.

Usisng foreign language skills as a Special Agent in an investigative capacity may pove satisfying for those interested in public service work, work that is potentially dangerous but always challenging.

Positions for nonagent personnel are also available in the Bureau. One of these positions is translator and interpreter. To be a candidate for this position one must be a U.S. citizen, a high school graduate for stationing anywhere in the U.S. or Puerto Rico. Applicants must pass a number of tests and undergo a formal interview. Proficiency in English, both spoken and written, must be demonstrated.

The FBI is constantly on the lookout for translators with language ability in the Romance, Germanic, Slavic, Arabic, or Oriental languages. Translators working for the FBI are expected to act also as interpreters. As a translating and interpreting a large portion of one's job consists of translating and interpreting written and oral foreign-language material into English. One would also be expected to translate and interpret from English into the foreign language in question. Interpreting for FBI officials would form a part of this work.

Most translators work in the Washington, D.C. area, but it is not impossible to be stationed in one of the FBI's field offices located throughout the country, especially those in major cities such as Chicago, New York, and San Francisco.

Translators start at the GS-5, 7, or 9 salary level. GS-5 is $15,738, GS-7 is $19,493, and GS-9 is $23,843. The salary level is usually determined by degree of experience: GS-7, one year of experience translating or interpreting, completion of one year of graduate study in the foreign language, or one year studying in a foreign university where the language of instruction is the foreign language in question; GS-9, two years' experience in translating or interpreting, or a master's degree in a foreign language, or a master's degree from a foreign university where the language of instruction is the foreign language in question. The basic qualification for the starting GS-5 is proficiency in one or more foreign languages acquired either through attendance at a high school where the foreign language concerned was the language of instruction, or living or working where the foreign language was the prevailing language. Alternatives are proficiency acquired through attendance at a four-year college or university with a major in the foreign language, and three years' experience translating and interpreting or other work requiring proficiency in English and another language.

It should be mentioned that all successful applicants are the thoroughly investigated by the FBI to determine their bakground and suitability for employment.

Interested students should write for further information to:

Federal Bureau of Investigation
Correspondents Unit
10th and Pennsylvania Ave
Washington, DC 20535

or phone the nearest office as listed in your telephone directory.

Central Intelligence Agency

The CIA is responsible for collecting, evaluating, and producing foreign intelligence. The information the Agency obtains is vital in providing a sound basis upon which senior U.S. policy-makers can make decisions regarding both the national security and develpments abroad. The Agency is concerned with gathering facts and making projections based on those facts, but not advocating one policy as opposed to another.

Given the nature of the Agency's activities and the worldwide scope in which it must operate, one can well imagine how large an organization it is and how many people are involved in various capacities to deal with the huge amount of intelligence material collected.

The CIA employs qualified people in almost every discipline, from economists and engineers to linguists and mathematicians. Certain jobs such as Intelligence Analyst require a broad range of knowledge in economics, politics, and military science. The process at work here is one of integration, evaluation, and analysis of data collected from diverse sources into a coherent whole, a brief report or lengthy study.

There are numerous opportunities for linguists in the CIA. A career opportunity pamphlet says, ''The Central Intelligence Agency offers exceptional employment opportunities for persons interested in foreign affairs and the use and cultivation of foreign languages. Assignments involve monitoring publications or conducting language training. Employees are offered the opportunity to work daily on tasks responsive to international events and to develop expert language skills.''

Language officers monitor foreign media—books, newspapers, and periodicals—to select and translate items significant to intelligence analysts and policymakers. Language officers are assigned to monitor one country or a group of countries or the developments in one particular topic area within a country, coordinating their work with intelligence analysts in specialized fields.

The CIA employs language teachers on a full- and part-time basis. Teachers must have native or near-native proficiency and extensive teaching experience. There are also job openings for PhD's in linguistics or foreign-language training who have teaching experience and proficiency in at least one language. Teachers work as staff in the CIA's Language School. Opportunities are provided for research in foreign-language pedagogy.

There is a particular need for people with high to native proficiency in Russian, Central Asian, Eastern European, Middle Eastern, and

Oriental languages. Proficiency in Scandinavian and Romance languages in combinations of two or more also consistitute eligibility.

Starting salaries range from GS-7 to GS-11 ($19,493 to $28,852) and sometimes higher, depending on qualifications, experience, and openings.

Those interested in obtaining more information, should write:

> Central Intelligence Agency.
> Personnel Representative
> Washington, DC 20505

Those interested in applying should send their résumés to:

> Department A
> P.O. Box 1925
> Washington, DC 20013

Peace Corps

The Peace Corps, in existence for over twenty years, was created as a means of helping Third World nations through people-to-people cooperation. More than 120,000 Americans have served in over sixty-six countries. Peace Corps volunteers work shoulder to shoulder with people in the local community, living with them, sharing themselves. Building houses and dams, sinking wells, helping with business administration, nursing, and teaching are activities that allow American volunteers to share what they know and to learn in turn what the people of other countries have to share. The Peace Corps experience is very must one of intercultural exchange. The basic principle behind the Corps is to add to local effort, not to override it, helping people to help themselves.

Any U.S. citizen over eighteen years of age and in good health is eligible to join the Peace Corps. Practical experience is desired, but no special degree is necessary. The Peace Corps provides training in whatever skills are needed. During a ten- to twelve-week training program, volunteers learn about the country to which they will go, as wellas being instructed in the language.

Volunteers with experience in environmental work such as foresters, fishery specialists, and agriculturals are needed. Volunteers with degrees or experience in architecture, science, engineering, and health are also highly appreciated.

The salary pad to volunteers will not make anyone rich. Money is somehow not the point. One receives a living allowance that covers housing, food, essentials, and a little pocket money. This usually comes to $9,000 for a typical two-year assignment.

Naturally, knowledge of the language of the country where you'll be serving is a necessity. If you don't speak that language, don't worry. The Peace Corps will teach you. Here's what a Peace Corps pamphlet says about foreign language:

> The challenge of learning a new language is demanding, absorbing and 24-hour work. Supportive and individualized Peace Corps language training through a ten- to twelve-week program provides each volunteer with a good start towards language proficiency.

The Peace Corps isn't for everyone. There are probably much easier ways to utilize the language skills you have. Still, if the idea of helping people and learning new things both about yourself and other peoples is appealing, the Peace Corps might be for you.

For more information, write:

> The Peace Corps
> Recruitment, 5th floor
> 1990 K Street NW
> Washington, DC 20526

or phone toll-free (800) 424-8580.

VISTA

According to a VISTA spokesperson, "VISTAs, Volunteers in Service to America, work together with rural and urban poor to find innovative solutions to community problems. VISTAs may work with grassroots organizations, nonprofit institutions or social service agencies helping others help themselves while living in the communities they serve."

VISTA could perhaps be called America's domestic Peace Corps. Both are indeed part of the same organiztion, ACTION (The Agency for Volunteer Service). VISTA needs skilled volunteers usually in the fields of community service, economic development, teaching, health, nutrition, legal rights, housing, and energy conservation.

There are no foreign-language requirements to serve with VISTA, nor does VISTA offer language instruction. Nonetheless language skills have proved a very important asset in many projects. This is so particularly in urban ethnic communities where English is often not spoken. In New York City, for example, working in Spanish-speaking neithborhoods, Chinatown, Italian communities, and areas where East European immigrants have settled usually requires language skills to be effective. Teaching English, helping people apply for needed services, assisting them through the bureaucratic maze of immigration and naturalization, and helping with housing and employment are projects that in a given community might require fluency in another language.

Service in VISTA is for a year or more. Applicants must be over eighteen years of age. At the moment, about 2,000 volunteers are serving. Some 50 percent of volunteers are assigned to projects in their own communities.

Other national volunteers groups include Action (476,000 volunteers), Foster Grandparent Program (20,700 volunteers), RSVP, Retired Senior Volunteer Program (401,300 volunteers), Senior Companion Program (9,200 volunteers), NCSL, National Center for Service Learning, and OVL, Office of Volunteer Liaison.

For more information write your nearest Vista/Action recruitment office or phone toll-free (800) 424-8867.

Military Service

Some students consider the military a career in which they can makes use of their language skill or acquire new languages through training. It is possible to receive language training, but it is not a decision that can be made solely by the individual. The military section to which one is assigned, whether it be in the Army, Air Force, Navy, or Marines, whether in communications, intelligence, supply, or documents, determines the need for capability in a foreign language and arranges that the necessary training be provided. Personnel working in a particular job where another language is required, and who are deemed suitable candidates for language training, undergo a language examination, the results of which decide whether or not they will be sent to the appropriate institution for instruction.

Most members of the military in need of language training receive it at the Defense Language Institute Foreign Language Center in Monterey, California. Another institute that provides language training to military personnel is the Foreign Service Institute in Washington, D.C.

For more information about foreign languages and the military, write or call the nearest local recruitment office in the branch of the military that interests you.

Local Government

The need for foreign language skills in local government most frequently arises in the area of social services provided by the municipal authority. Those who could benefit most from another language are case workers in agencies that serve ethnic communities where a language other than English is spoken by a good many of the people. Most U.S. cities offer extensive social services and have a corresponding staff, though sometimes not sufficient to meet the volume of work. Major urban centers have a particularly wide range of services. With the majority of non-English speakers tending to congregate in these urban centers, the demand for bilingual and multilingual staff is great. New York City, for example, known as the melting pot of the nation, has services including a bureau of child support, day-care programs, dental health centers, departments of family, adult, and senior citizen services, medical assistance, and many more. A public affairs officer of the New York Social Services information office said that the last group of caseworkers recently hired were all bilingual in English and Spanish.

Qualifications for these jobs vary with the job and the local government. Those interested in obtaining more information should write to the department of personnel or human resources of their municipality.

Chapter VI

Communications and the Media

Radio and Television

In the field of radio, foreign language skills are most valuable with the Voice of America, the global radio network of the United States Information Agency, and with the private organization Radio Free Europe/Radio Liberty Inc.

The goal of the Voice of America (VOA) is to promote understanding of America to people abroad through a wide range of programs on cultural, political, social, and economic matters. The VOA also broadcasts objective news reports on world events. In 1976 the U.S. Congress passed new legislation covering the Voice of America. The following are the principles governing OVA broadcasts:

(1) VOA will serve as a consistently reliable and authoritative source of news. VOA news will be accurate, objective, and comprehensive.

(2) VOA will represent America, not any single segment of American society, and will therefore present a balanced and comprehensive projection of significant American thought and institutions.

(3) VOA will present the policies of the United States clearly and effectively, and will also present responsible discussion and opinion on these policies.

The VOA regularly schedules broadcasts in forty-three languages as well as presenting special programs in other languages. The VOA has 1,200 hours of direct broadcast per week of programs prepared by VOA and broadcast by local radio stations in other countries.

Jobs with the VOA are as adapters and announcers in the various branches of the organization. The work consists of translating and adapting English-language programs prapared in Washington that cover science, economics, politics, and world news. Adapters-translators are responsible for tailoring these scripts to meet local tastes in style and presentation as well as condensing them to meet time specifications.

Adapters/translators sometimes have the opportunity to write scripts of their own on a wide range of subjects that will provide an illuminating view of various aspects of America. Staff members must keep informed of developments in the areas to which they are broadcasting.

Only people with experience in working and communicating in a foreign language will be considered. They must have wide knowledge of the affairs of the target area to which the broadcasts are made. Skill in radio writing is essential. The candidate must have a voice appropriate for international broadcasting. Tests are given in these various areas.

Since the VOA operates seven days a week twenty-four hours a day, staff members must be prepared to work according to programming schedules.

Listed below are the languages in which broadcasting occurs:

Albanian	Georgian	Portuguese
Amharic	Greek	Romanian
Arabic	Hausa	Russian
Armenian	Hindi	Serbo-Croatian
Azerbaijoni	Hungarian	Slovak
Bengali	Indonesian	Solvenian
Bulgarian	Khmer	Spanish
Burmeses	Korean	Swahili
Chinese	Lao	Thai
Creole	Latvian	Turkish
Czech		

Dari	Lithuanian	Ukrainian
English	Pashto	Urdu
Estonian	Persian	Uzbek
French	Polish	Vietnamese

To apply, one must fill out a Personal Qualifications Statement, SF-171, and send it to:

USIA-Voice of America
Office of Personnel
Room 1526
330 Independence Avenue
Washington, DC 20547

Salaries as an international radio broadcaster (foreign languages) range from are $23,000 at GS-9 and $28,000 at GS-11 and up, depending upon qualifications.

Radio Free Europe reaches approximately 38 million people in Eastern Europe, and Radio Liberty reaches more than 15 million people in the USSR. From 1950 and 1951, when RFE and RL respectively were founded, until 1971 the bulk of RFE/RL financing came from the CIA. Today, after a reorganization, the Presidentially appointed Board of International Broadcasting audits Congressional funding of RFE/RL. Although RFE/RL is an independent professional organization, it is required by law to operate "in a manner not inconsistent with the broad foreign policy objectives of the United States."

Radio Liberty broadcasts in fifteen of the languages spoken in the USSR. Radio Free Europe broadcasts in six major languages of Eastern Europe. Following is a list of languages and an approximation of the number of hours of daily broadcast in each:

Radio Free Europe

Bulgarian	8
Czech and Slovak	21½
Hungarian	18½

Polish	19¾
Romanian	12¾

Radio Liberty
Slovak:

Russian	24
Ukrainian	10
Belorussian	3

Caucasian:

Armenian	3
Azeri	4
Georgian	3

Baltic:

Estonian	3
Latvian	3
Lithuanian	3
Tatar-Bashkir	3

Turkestani:

Kazak	3
Kirghiz	1
Tajik	1¼
Turkmen	1
Uzbek	3¾

Programs are prepared by professional staff journalists assisted by the major press services and researchers working in unique archives in this field. Each staff member is assigned to a desk according to area of expertise. Free-lance writers and broadcasters play an important part in RFE/RL. Emigrés and exiles form the greatest part of the free-lance staff. Writing and broadcasting in their native language, they often discuss books, music, and political events. Ninety percent of RFE/RL's programs are produced at the Munich headquarters, where 1,000 of their 1,700 employees work.

The programming center and headquarters of RFE/RL are in Munich, Germany. There are also news bureaus in London, Paris, Brussels, Bonn, and Rome. The corporate, fiscal, and U.S. liaison headquarters is in Washington, D.C. Other program centers are located in New York and Washington, with a separate news bureau in Washington. Transmitters are located in Germany, Portugal, and Spain. The overwhelming majority of staff is located in Munich.

Students of Slavic studies programs interested in working for RFE/RL can participate in an eight- to twelve-week internship program in Munich. Application should be to:

> RFE/RL
> Oettingen STR. 67
> Am Englischen Garten
> 8000 München 22
> West Germany

Those interested in a permanent position can write to the same address or:

> Personnel Director
> RFE/RL
> 1201 Connecticut Ave. NW
> Washington, DC 20036

Recruitment often takes place at various Slavic studies conventions such as the meeting of the Association for the Advancement of Slavic Studies. Advertisements of openings also appear in various Slavic studies journals.

In radio and television programs for domestic consumption there is obviously less need for producers, broadcasters, performers, and writers to have knowledge of foreign languages. A growing trend, however, seems to indicate that need for language skills among staff in radio and television will increase as new programs are developed to attract an audience composed of ethnic groups. Cable television has launched a number of programs in Spanish. Some radio stations provide language instruction programs in addition to the general entertainment fare broadcast in other languages.

The growth area in these media as regards foreign languages is definitely in cable television. Already there are networks that show only Spanish-language programs. Others broadcast special programs in Japanese and Chinese. Clearly, these networks are trying to capture the ethnic market in the large urban areas, a segment of the population that had previously been cut off from the mass media precisely because of the language barrier. The need for radio and television writers and programmers with a knowledge of the language of their target audience will be very great indeed.

The Film Industry

The film industry is very much an international one. Italian directors collaborate with Swedish cameramen in filming a mixed cast of Americans, Germans, Poles, and Spaniards. Clearly in an industry where such specialized skills as acting, filming, directing, editing, and writing are in demand and where intense scrutiny is given those skills before the selection of a person, the knowledge of a foreign language is not usually a decisive factor as to whether one lands a job. Still, considering the increased ease with which one can work internationally, ability in a second or third language should not be underestimated. There is no doubt that an actor or actress would bring more to a part in a film shot on location if he or she had knowledge of the place, of the culture, and ideally of the language. Filmmakers who choose as their subject some aspect of another culture, whether it be a documentary about the architecture of Leningrad or an original script based on an Italian political scandal, would be able to do more thorough research and produce a more insightful film if they knew the language of the country in question. In addition to the advantages inherent in knowing one's subject in greater depth as a result of language skills, there is also the necessity of communicating that knowledge to others involved in the actual making of the film. When dealing with an international crew and cast of actors and actresses, communication is to say the least essential; by limiting the number of misunderstandings and increasing the likelihood of intentions being grasped, ability to speak other languages benefits everyone present.

The most direct application of foreign languages to film, however, is in the writing of subtitles. Foreign films imported to the U.S. and American films exported for distribution abroad both require this process. Dubbing is almost never done in the U.S. The American public is now accustomed to seeing foreign films with subtitles. American films distributed abroad, particularly to Spain and South America, are sometimes dubbed, but the dubbing is done abroad by actors of the country.

Most of the major film companies do their own subtitling in-house for distribution abroad. One or two administrators usually supervise the work of free-lancers. Since the American companies make films in English, the free-lancers who do the subtitling are usually native speakers of the language into which the film is subtitled. For instance, Paramount pictures distributes films to South America. The films that require subtitles in Portuguese are usually handled by a number of Brazilian journalists living in New York. Those to be distributed to Mexico, Argentina, and other Spanish-speaking countries are subtitled by native Spanish speakers who are scrupulous in rendering the dialogue into a neutral Spanish; that is, avoiding regional idiomatic expressions that would limit distribution.

Americans with knowledge of foreign languages can work free-lance subtitling foreign films into English. There are not many jobs to be had, but whatever work there is comes from American distributors handling foreign films.

The going rate for subtitling is between $85 and $120 per reel. An average feature film has ten to twelve reels.

Publishing

Book publishing is a difficult field to enter. Many people consider it one of the most interesting of professions. Anybody interested in reading and writing, in literature of all kinds, thinks—and perhaps rightly so—that publishing would be an area in which they could fulfill themselves, dealing as they would with things they like. Since there a multitude of readers and would-be writers in the world, however, there is a great deal of competition for jobs in publishing.

Knowledge of a foreign language is an asset in the world of publishing, especially as publishing is becoming more and more an international endeavor every year. Foreign rights, previously neglected in large part by American publishers, are now a very important part of the business. Coproduction between American and European publishers on particularly costly projects is also finding more and more favor. Many of these deals are made during the international book fairs, which are held yearly. The one in Frankfurt, Germany, is the oldest and most famous, but there are also fairs in Jerusalem, Mexico City, and Bologna.

Since book publishers are constantly looking for and finding books written by foreign authors and published abroad, there is a need for qualified translators. Few publishing houses have an in-house staff of translators. Translators are usually hired on a free-lance basis for a specific project.

In many cases, particularly with fiction and poetry, the translation is as important as the book itself. Given this fact, publishing houses usually look for translators with a reputation in the field. Often the translators are noted authors in their own right. For this reason, it is not easy to get books to translate. A good contact with an editor at one of the publishing houses helps a great deal. Another method of operating is to bring to the attention of an editor a work in a foreign language that you think would be successful in the U.S. and that has never been translated into English and offer to translate the book. It would be to your advantage to find out the status of the book's foreign rights, perhaps to correspond with the author and ask if he or she is interested in seeing the work translated into English. All this takes time, and sometimes it is very difficult to get the information you want. In addition to this, getting a publishing house interested in the book is often as difficult as it is to persuade a house to publish your own work. Translators working on a book for a publishing company sometimes are paid a flat fee, but it is preferable to obtain a royalty agreement; 5 percent is an average figure.

Most large publishing houses have a department devoted entirely to foreign rights. Though English is the language of international business, it is a tremendous help—some would say a necessity—in the area of foreign rights to be able to speak a number of languages. The people in foreign rights basically buy from publishers abroad the right to sell their books in the United States or whatever territory is stipulated by the agreement and sell to publishers abroad the foreign rights of the books they publish in the U.S. Besides having the business sense to work out a profitable deal, people in foreign rights need a good sense both about books and the markets where they can be sold. A knowledge of other countries, cultures, and languages is essential when trying to choose books from one's list that would be suitable for sale in Germany, for example, or Italy. Often your opposite numbers in rights will rely on your judgment in buying. Similarly, you will find yourself relying on them for advice on which books to purchase from their lists. Ability to communicate in the language of your counterpart in these matters makes for a warmth and trust that might be difficult to obtain otherwise.

Editors and production staff both would do well to be able to operate in more than one language. As mentioned earlier, American publishing companies often team up with European ones to jointly produce new books, sharing costs and collaborating editorially. The difficulties of operating internationally are sufficiently great no matter what the complexity of the project, so that the easier it is to communicate, the better the results.

With the rising costs of printing in the U.S., many publishers are having work done abroad, particularly in Hong Kong, Taiwan, and Korea, as well as in certain plants in Italy, Spain, and the Netherlands.

Though most of these companies are able to conduct their correspondence in English, when trying to evaluate the compatibility of the project with the equipment, it would stand your company in good stead if on the technical level you were able to speak and write in the necessary language, thus avoiding many of the misunderstandings that frequently occur in these dealings.

The editorial staff of a publishing house needs a wide range of knowledge in many areas because of the diversity of the material they handle. People in publishsign still talk about "the cultured individual," someone with sufficient sophistication to be able to judge quality in books, advertising, design, whatever. In accordance with the European conception of a "cultured individual," many executives in publishsing regard knowledge of languages as an essential attribute. Whether dealing with foreign authors, foreign-language textbooks, or the odd foreign phrase inthe body of an English text, the editor or assistant editor with foreign language skills will be regarded as that much more competent as a result of his or her language ability.

Salaries in publishing vary greatly depending on one's experience and position. Entry-level positions could start as low as $13,000; a top editor could make as much as $150,000.

Journalism

Journalism is a profession that demands many skills and instincts: the ability to write well and quickly, follow up leads, get to the bottom of a matter, report accurately. Knowledge of a foreign language has not been considered a must for journalists, although no one would deny that it is an asset.

The need for foreign language skills arises in a number of circumstances. In the United States, a reporter might have to cover a story that occurred in a Spanish-speaking community. Getting statements, conducting interviews, trying to find out what happened, would be greatly facilitated if the reporter spoke Spanish. Investigative reporting is difficult enough; a language barrier is one more impediment to a reporter. Salespeople in the advertising department of a newspaper that has a wide circulation among spanish-speakers sometimes find themselves selling space to Spanish-speaking advertisers. Knowledge of Spanish can increase sales, make transactions easier.

Obviously, the majority of the occasions when a bilingual or multilingual journalist will feel a particular advantage will be abroad. Journalists who cover the news abroad are called foreign correspondents. It is amazing how many foreign correspondents don't speak another language, let alone the language of the country to which they're assigned. The majority do not, and yet the need is so great. Most foreign correspondents have to rely on readers to tell them what the local papers are reporting; readers are bilingual nationals who work as staff in the bureau of the news agency in their country. In addition to readers, correspondents rely largely on press conferences at which official statements are released and the usual question and answer period follows. Interpreters are present at these sessions when necessary. Apart from these two methods of obtaining news, foreign correspondents who are not proficient in the language in question must rely on interpreters to accompany them on any investigative project they undertake; that or the unsatisfactory expedient of hoping that the people one needs to interview speak English.

Journalists themselves are not really to blame in all this. Many editors have felt and still feel that a good journalist can cover the news anywhere, that the journalistic method is such that it can be applied in any country and potentially cover any subject. Journalists are not meant to be experts in an area. There have been instances of ''old China hands,'' journalists with a knowledge of Chinese and fifteen years' experience in the country, who have been transferred home to edit the literary section or cover national politics. Foreign correspondents are often moved from country to country after an assignment has been completed.

There is some indication that journalism's attitude toward foreign languages is changing. This may be the result of the increased competitiveness involved in the job market. Whatever skills one has besides first-rate journalistic ones could become decisive in securing a position. Someone with proficiency in Russian has a far better chance of being sent to a Moscow bureau than someone without.

A posting to the Middle East is far more likely—all other things being equal—if the journalist knows Arabic. In addition to pure language skill, area specialization is also an advantage.

Students wishing to pursue journalism careers should enroll in an advanced-degree program in journalism. The Columbia University School of Journalism is considered by many to be one of the finest in the U.S. Though there are no foreign-language requirements for entry into the program, knowledge of another language is considered an asset. In the Ohio State master's degree program in journalism, however, you must be fluent in at least one language and also must spend a six-month internship in the part of the world where you would like to be a correspondent.

Journalists' salaries vary greatly. An entry-level position could pay $15,000 per annum whereas someone with a number of years' experience could earn $35,000 or more.

Chapter **VII**

Other Career Options

One of the benefits of studying foreign languages is the great number of career options available to you, combining your language skill with the skills required for work in a field that interests you. In some of the fields discussed in this chapter, the application of foreign languages to the work is direct and immediate; in others, the connection is more oblique. Some of the jobs mentioned are not full time; others will make up your work life. Though the various jobs discussed do not form an all-inclusive list of jobs in which foreign languages can be utilized, those dealt with give more than just an indication of the range available.

Tourism and Travel

Tourism is a growth industry. More people are traveling than ever before. The reasons are numerous. The world seems a smaller place, connected as it is by rapid transit and communication. Travel is less expensive, and people are more knowledgeable about faraway places and thus more curious to see them. International business and trade has also played a part in making people travel and forcing them to think internationally.

Travel and tourism are largely a question of economics. Fluctuations in currencies make some countries less expensive than others. At one point devaluation of the dollar caused millions of foreign tourists to visit the United States. When the dollar is strong, Americans tend to travel abroad in greater numbers. Besides the bargains weak currencies provide, charter flights and the competition among airlines stimulate travel. Package holidays also provide opportunities to travel for many vacationers who otherwise could not afford it. These packages include the price of the flight, hotel, and usually one meal in an all-inclusive price that is considerably lower than if these things were paid for separately.

To serve the ever-growing number of visitors to the U.S., the so-called hospitality industries have increased. The hotel, motel, and restaurant businesses account for a large portion of the dollar volume in this industry. Airline companies have also benefited tremendously from the tourist boom. Tourist agencies providing sightseeing excursions and other guided tours and arranging travel and hotel accommodations are also an integral part of the industry.

There are jobs in all of these businesses that require people with foreign language skills. One of the greatest fears of foreign travelers to the U.S. is the language barrier they know they will encounter if they themselves do not speak English. Americans have a reputation for speaking no other languages, and foreign visitors have terrible visions of getting lost or boarding the wrong bus and being unable to communicate and ask for directions or help. Staff in hotels, airlines, and tour agencies that have frequent dealings with foreign visitors are expected to know more than just English.

The United States Travel and Tourism Administration, a branch of the Department of Commerce, in efforts to stimulate travel to the United States, has made attempts to alleviate some of the language difficulties that foreign visitors encounter. One of its programs is the Gateway Reception Service. The program was created to welcome international tourists and business persons requiring assistance with Federal inspection formalities. At present, about 230 Gateway Receptionists are stationed in New York, Seattle, San Juan, Philadelphia, Miami, Boston, Bangor, Los Angeles, Honolulu, Atlanta, New Orleans, and Baltimore. Most of the receptionists are bilingual or multilingual college students on Work-Study Programs or part- and full-time employees of airports or convention and visitors bureaus. Interpreters serve in twenty-seven languages, ranging from Spanish, French, German, and Japanese to Serbo-Croatian, Hindi, and Urdu. The United States Travel and Tourism Administration is appropriated funds by Congress. In addition, convention centers, visitor bureaus, and airports supply financing.

Those wishing to obtain more information about the U.S. Travel and Tourism Administration should write to:

> U.S. Department of Commerce
> U.S. Travel and Tourism Administration
> Washington, DC 20230

The airlines also are aware of the difficulties foreign travelers can meet when leaving and entering the country. Passenger service staff of many of the major airlines are expected to know other languages. Some do not, but others know as many as five or six languages. Passenger service staff work in ticketing or as ground hosts. In both jobs one works constantly with the public. With such a large amount of international travel, a good portion of that public may be people who do not speak English. Selling tickets, checking passengers in, and making seating arrangements are all jobs that someone in passenger service must do. The job is easier, the work done more efficiently, and the public relations for the airline done better if the staff member can work in another language when the occasion demands. Ground hosts deal with customer complaints, flight changes, missed flights, and other problems that have to be handled when the passenger is on the ground.

The airlines provide on-the-job training for these positions. Applicants should apply directly to the personnel department of the various airline companies, including a résumé. Staff in passenger service make in salary anywhere between $440 and $600 per week, depending on job level and number of years of experience.

Another job with the airlines where foreign-language skill is usually required is that of flight attendant, otherwise known as steward or stewardess. Flight attendants are responsible for inflight service to passengers. Their duties are fairly well known to anyone who has traveled by air: checking galley and cabins to make sure all equipment and food is on board, helping to seat passengers and to stow hand luggage, checking seat belts, demonstrating safety equipment, making announcements over the public address system, serving food and refreshments, administering first aid when necessary, and others.

Flight attendants average seventy-five flying hours a month. Working hours vary according to duration and schedule of flights. On the average, a flight attendant works fifteen days a month and then has fifteen days off.

Applicants for a flight attendant's position must be at least eighteen years of age and in good health, fulfill certain height and weight requirements, have at least a high school diploma or the equivalent, and be mature, responsible, and outgoing. Airlines that fly international routes usually require flight attendants to be fluent in at least one foreign language.

Salaries for flight attendants vary from airline to airline. Generally speaking, salaries start at $1,346 a month for sixty-five hours, and overtime is paid at about $23.81 an hour. Dependent on position and experience, salaries increase. For instance, a cabin attendant on a domestic flight working sixty-five hours a month can expect to make $2,236 a month after twelve years, and a service manager on international flights may expect to make from $2,600 to $2,800 a month as base pay after six years.

Most airline companies run their own training programs for flight attendants. These courses usually run for four weeks, providing instruction in emergency and safety procedures, first aid, airline procedures, and many other necessary skills. Some training facilities have language laboratories for trainees and staff to brush up on their language skills. Upon successful completion of the training programs, new flight attendants are sent to work on a six-month trial.

Those interested in obtaining application forms should write to the Director of Flight Service at the headquarters of the airlines in which they're interested.

The Hotel and Motel Industry

When travelers first arrive at a destination at which they intend to stay for a time, the first thing they have to think about is accommodations. The hotel and motel industry serves this need. Providing rooms and services to travelers be they tourists or businessmen can be big business, depending on the size of the operation.

Running a hotel or motel is no easy matter; the bigger the establishment, the greater the complexity. Making sure the maximum number of rooms are booked without overbooking, buying and preparing food and drink, housekeeping, billing, accounting, supervising staff, arranging for advertising are all specialized jobs that require training and experience. All the work of the hotel is geared toward one goal: satisfying the guest, providing him or her with any help or service needed.

Foreign-language ability is a very important skill for some members of the staff. In an attempt to be as helpful as possible to guests, the staff should be prepared to deal on many different professional levels in another language should the need arise. Hotels by their very nature have a diverse clientele; foreign guests, especially in urban centers, are by no means the exception.

There are many positions in the field of hotel administration: General Manager, Front Office Manager, Director of Guests, Food and Beverage Manager, Banquet Manager, Sales, Public Relations, and many more. Those jobs that require the staff to deal extensively with the public often must be filled by people who are bilingual or multilingual. If one is working for an international hotel with establishments all over the world, foreign-language skill is a tremendous asset in the organization no matter what one's managerial position. The reason for this is that one could well be assigned to one of the organization's hotels in Cairo or Paris or elsewhere, and in dealing with staff that is locally hired as well as the public at large, foreign language skills are a necessity.

Most large hotel organizations run their own management training programs. Recruits are taken either from the ranks of the nonmanagerial staff who show particular aptitude and potential, or from a college that offers a BA in hotel management. It is also possible to apply directly to these training programs from college, not necessarily with a hotel degree. Foreign-language skills are not a prerequisite for admission, but such skills are a definite advantage.

Below are listed three well-known colleges that offer degrees in hotel management.

Florida International University
School of Hospitality Management
Broward Center
3501 SW Davie Road
Fort Lauderdale, FL 33314

Cornell University
School of Hotel Administration, Statler Hall
Ithaca, NY 14853-6901

University of Houston–University Park
Conrad Hilton College
4800 Calhoun
Hoston, TX 77004

Major hotel chains such as Hilton, Sheraton, and Hyatt, which have their own training programs, can be contacted directly by writing to the personnel department at their headquarters.

Salaries in the hotel industry vary widely with the job. Someone starting in a front-office job should expect to make about $20,000 per year. A top managerial position could pay as much as $65,000 per year.

Though language skills are no guarantee that one is going to climb the advancement ladder in the hotel industry, they are skills that certainly increase one's usefulness and worldwide mobility. Promotion, as in any field, is based on the work one does. Whatever extra ability one has that assists him or her in that work, so much the better.

Tour Personnel

The travel industry provides a good many opportunities for people with language skills. Tour operators, tour managers, and local tour guides all have occasion in the performance of their professional duties to utilize their knowledge of other languages. Tour operators put together package holidays. In their capacity as travel agents it is necessary to deal with hotels and sometimes their own counterparts all over the world. Though English is the international language of business, knowledge of a foreign language can be helpful in establishing personal contacts abroad. In addition to this, a travel agent is clearly more effective if he or she is personally acquainted with the country or countries in question. Being able to speak the language of the country in question is an excellent indication to a client of one's expertise. Language ability would also help a tour operator who catered to a particular ethnic clientele. If one's offices, for example, were located in a Hispanic neighborhood, a knowledge of Spanish would help one's business; that and offering special tours to Puerto Rico and Mexico would make good business sense.

Tour managers are professional travel escorts. They are the on-the-spot representatives of the company that has organized the tour. They need considerable skill in dealing with people both as individuals and as a group, knowledge of travel procedures such as those involved in ticketing and scheduling, familiarity with the locale so as to be able to guide and advise tour participants, and ability to act as interpreter when the need arises. Tour managers act in two liaison capacities: one between the tour company and tour participants and one between the tour participants and the world in which they're traveling. Knowledge of foreign languages, then, is a very necessary ability for the tour manager to have. If he or she is taking a group abroad, the group will rely on the tour manager to handle and oversee customs and immigration procedures and hotel and airline check-ins in whatever language is called for. Tour managers sometimes act in the capacity of local guide, meeting a group of foreign tourists for their trip around the United States. In this case, ability to speak the language of the group is absolutely essential.

Many tour managers are not professionals. Tour organizers often advertise positions available in the spring for a summer tour. These positions are often filled by teachers on vacation who are suitable in many respects, most particularly for their experience with group movement.

Tour managers are usually paid on a per diem basis. Those just entering the field make between $35 and $50 a day plus expenses. More seasoned managers have been known to make up to $200 a day plus expenses.

Local tour guides work on a free-lance basis, having connections with a number of tour companies. As a rule, they are experts in the history, legends, and monuments of a given place, a city or a village or even a natural monument. They work in conjunction with the tour manager, staying with the group just long enough to complete a guided tour. Local guides in the U.S. need foreign-language skills in order to lead foreign tourists on sight seeing excursions. The more languages they know, the greater the number of jobs that will be available to them. Local tour guides are paid on a per diem basis, usually between $80 and $150 plus expenses and tips.

Most cities exert some control over the people who act as guides. In order to protect tourists from charlatans who make up history as they go along, most cities require those who want to be guides to take an examination. This examination is usually administered by the consumer affairs department of local government. In New York City the fee to take the exam is $50.

How does one become a tour manager or local guide? Most people come to the profession from related jobs like front-desk work at an airline or travel agency. Some tour operators train their own people. Some local guides are self-taught. There are various schools that train tour managers and local guides. One of the more respected schools is the American Tour Management Institute in New York. Their Certificate of Completion has gained considerable recognition by the trade. To receive the certificate you must be eighteen years of age and have a high school diploma or an equivalency certificate. Interested students should write to:

> American Tour Management Institute
> Suite 1403
> 271 Madison Avenue
> New York, NY 10016

Law

Lawyers who have language skills increase their effectiveness in handling international legal matters. Corporate lawyers representing large firms that do extensive trade overseas can use their foreign language knowledge to negotiate in disputes with foreign executives, draw up contracts, and advise on international trade agreements. International lawyers can represent the interests of foreign clients in this country. A lawyer with a reputation for proficiency in this or that language will attract a much larger clientele from among foreign firms because of the ability to communicate with them in their own language. The confidence inspired by fluency in the language of one's client is incalculable. Further, the saving in both time and money from being able to dispense with the services of a translator and interpreter is tremendous.

Lawyers whose offices serve the legal needs of specific ethnic communities need foreign language skills to deal with non-English-speaking clients. These language skills are particularly useful for lawyers working in legal aid, offering legal services to the poor and disenfranchised, many of whom are recent immigrants without knowledge of English.

Entrance to law school is largely based on a student's college record, educational background, and work experience, and the law school admissions examination LSAT. Law schools show a preference for students who have had a broad liberal arts training rather than narrow specialization. Candidates for law school are evaluated on their reading and writing ability, their facility with spoken English, and their ability to think logically and critically. Undergraduate study of foreign languages is considered a very good background for law school.

A good reference book for those interested in opportunities in international law is the *Directory of Opportunities in International Law*. This can be obtained from the John Bassett Moore Society of International Law, University of Virginia School of Law, Charlottesville, VA 22901.

Library Science

A master's degree in library science is necessary to work as a librarian. Most programs require candidates to be proficient in at least one foreign language. The reason for this is simple: librarians in the course of their work handle numerous foreign-language books, newspapers, and periodicals. In order to catalog this material correctly, the librarian has to have an idea of subject matter. Reference librarians and archivists particularly benefit from knowledge of foreign languages, the more the better, so that they can provide access to documents and reference materials for students and scholars as required. Most public and college libraries have foreign-language literature collections. Librarians with language ability are needed to administer these. City libraries, particularly those located in an ethnic community of an urban center, have developed special collections and services for the members of the community. Librarians with the language capabilities to handle these collections and work with the reading public are very important. The need for Spanish-speaking ability is especially great in these libraries.

Majoring in a foreign language is an excellent undergraduate course of study for those interested in becoming librarians. There is a growing need for librarians with a knowledge of the less frequently studied languages such as Chinese, Japanese, and Arabic. Whatever language or languages one chooses to study as an undergraduate, that skill will be useful throughout one's career in libraries. It is also a qualification that increases one's employability, making the job hunt a little easier.

There are many other areas of work in which foreign-language skills are an asset and sometimes a necessity. Medicine is one such field. Doctors, nurses, even medical technologists, encounter many situations in which ability in another language helps them in their work. This is especially so in research, where specialists often have to read reports in other languages to keep up to date. Though most of these articles are translated into English, the process is sometimes slow, taking as long as a year. But foreign languages are not only useful in the rarefied atmosphere of published discoveries.

Medical personnel are discovering more and more the necessity of knowing another language in order to care for patients. This is particularly the case in hospitals and clinics that offer services to minority groups and recent immigrants who either do not know any English or do not know English well enough to describe their symptoms or understand what the medical staff says about tests and treatment. The rapid growth of the Spanish-speaking population throughout the United States has made Spanish the most needed second language for medical personnel. Positions for bilingual personnel are often listed in the classified section of Sunday newspapers in urban centers.

Scientists and social scientists also benefit in their work from knowledge of a foreign language. Scientists working in the various areas of science, be it chemistry, physics, or biology, like their counterparts in medicine, need foreign languages in order to read research articles written in other languages. Though over half the science articles published the world over are written in English, the majority of the remainder appear in Russian, German, and French. Many publications are either abstracted or translated in their entirety into English, but scientists who need to keep up to date with new developments cannot afford to wait for translations to appear, and to have translations done privately is very costly.

Social scientists such as sociologists, anthropologists, archeologists, and political scientists find knowledge of foreign languages a necessary skill for their work. Whether one is working as a sociologist studying social groups and the way they function in a particular environment or as an archeologist excavating the site of a buried city, knowledge of the languages in question brings a much increased depth of understanding about one's subject. This ought to be self-evident. A sociologist doing research on Turkish immigrants working in industrialized centers in West Germany would do well to know both German and Turkish; insights that could be gained through being able to speak to the people in their own language are tremendous. One's credibility is also enhanced.

Cultural anthropologists study people and their culture. Whether one is doing field work in the jungles of South America or the deserts of the Middle East, knowledge of the language of the people one is studying is essential. Anthropologists usually teach at colleges and universities, doing their own research when not in the field. As with any scholarly research, articles appear in a number of languages in professional journals. To keep abreast, ability to read in some of these foreign languages is very helpful. Field work might well entail living for extended periods with a tribe in their native habitat, and ability to communicate with them is mandatory.

Archeologists study ancient civilizations through the discovery and assembly of their artifacts, working all over the world. In order to communicate with the native population, contact with whom could range from colleagues at a university near the excavation site to local laborers acting as diggers, knowledge of the language in question is helpful. Knowledge of the language of the ancient civilization to which the research is directed is of course a necessity. Reading ability in other languages is useful for keeping abreast of discoveries by foreign colleagues who publish their findings in their own language. In the field of classical archeology, knowledge of German is very useful in this respect.

Political scientists need to know other languages in their study of government. National and international politics is an immensely complicated area of study. Whether one is a professor, a foreign service officer, or a researcher for a private organization, it is necessary to be familiar not only with the political system of a country but with its culture and language. Such knowledge provides the political scientist with a broader perspective on political events than he otherwise could have. It prevents viewing world events from a strictly American point of view, a fault that many political scientists see in political analysts in government. Many feel that our international problems could be ameliorated if our political specialists were more fully aware of the history and culture of the countries they deal with. Much of this understanding could be at least begun through knowing the languages of the countries being studied.

Those interested in pursuing a religious vocation will find that foreign-language skills are an asset in their studies. Jewish seminaries require students to know Hebrew. Knowledge of European languages is also helpful for scholarly work. Entry into the priesthood requires students to have a BA from a four-year college before attending another four years at a seminary. Knowledge of Latin is required, and depending upon one's course of study, be it scripture or theology, one might study biblical Greek, Hebrew, German, and French. Those interested in becoming Protestant ministers are advised to pursue a liberal arts degree in a four-year college before entering a theological seminary. A foreign language major would be well considered. Missionaries clearly need foreign-language skills since the basic aim of their work is to proselytize, that is, to convert people to their religion, as well as acting in various social service capacities. Most missionaries are instructed in the necessary language after assignment to a specific part of the world. Experience has shown, however, that knowing any other foreign language is tremendously helpful in learning a new one—and the difficulties of learning a new one are amplified when it may be an obscure African language—so the more languages one knows, the better. Communication is the most important part of the missionary's activities. To end with an interesting aside: Missionaries as a group have made great contributions to our knowledge of other languages, compiling the first dictionaries of a number of Asian and African languages.

Chapter VIII

Opportunities in the Nineties

The future for careers using foreign languages grows ever brighter as the world becomes more closely knit and moves toward the twenty-first century. With the help of such technologies as the telephone, fax machines, express mail, and other as yet unheard-of developments, the countries of the world are increasingly becoming bound together in trade and commerce. In mastering the language of one or more foreign countries, you will be able to take part in this intercultural revolution.

The Pacific Rim

"East is East, and West is West, and never the twain shall meet," wrote Rudyard Kipling. That once widely held view has given way to the realities of late twentieth-century economics. East and West are becoming increasingly interdependent. Among the northern countries of the Pacific Rim, Japan, China, and Taiwan have received the most attention. Since the Korean War, South Korea has become a significant economic entity. In addition, academics are interested in Vietnam and Cambodia, both of which have played a role in the shaping of American history.

Scholars have dubbed the 1980s the Age of the Pacific Basin. In 1981, noted scholar Yoshihiro Nakamura, American trade with the nations of the Pacific overtook the total value of trade with the nations of the Atlantic.

Perhaps the best-known Asian country to most Americans is Japan, which has become a major economic power. Our military enemy in

World War II, Japan has become our friendly competitor in world trade. Now highly prosperous, Japan has imported many elements of American commercialism, such as the Disneyland in Tokyo. Through their industrial system of loyalty and group effort, the Japanese have created a productive system that rivals that of the United States. The Japanese once sought to learn about American technologies. For example, the video cassette recorder (VCR) was invented in the United States and improved by the Japanese in the 1960s. Today, however, we could learn from them how to increase production in our factories by offering our workers the same sense of belonging and pride that the Japanese are able to instill in their workers. In fact, when in 1982 Congress was trying to improve the position of American companies in the world market, it used the Japanese export trading company Sogo Shosha as a model.

We often stress how much like us the Japanese are becoming when in actuality we are miles apart both literally and culturally. However, a translator or interpreter should find a reflection of cultural values in the language studied. It is far better to appreciate differences than to assume sameness. In studying Japanese, for instance, an English speaker will immediately realize the importance of hierarchy in Japanese society. One who wishes to command the language must be continually aware of the person being addressed and adjust the conjugation of verbs according to whether that person is superior, equal, or inferior to the speaker. Another interesting linguistic difference is that the subject of a Japanese sentence is often omitted and must be inferred. The structure of the English sentence is based on Latin grammar, in which the subject is explicitly stated. All these differences require a translator to be creative yet accurate in finding suitable expressions.

Since more people speak Japanese than other Asian languages, the competition is greater than that of, say, Chinese or Korean. The popularity of a language in the United States will depend on how we view our future political and economic relations with the country. In the case of Japan we can be fairly optimistic.

Although political considerations such as the recent government repression of the student movement for democratization in China may seem to bode ill for continued interaction, the economics of the China position has not ruled out continuing American participation in that country's economic growth. Even uncertainty about the future of Hong Kong when that British crown colony reverts to the People's Republic of China in 1997 does not lessen the need for those who can act as translators and interpreters. Most American businessmen hold that economic ties should be maintained and strengthened.

The Chinese language is difficult for English speakers at first because its objective is to achieve the maximum brevity of expression. It was not until the turn of the twentieth century that Chinese underwent a literary revolution and modern colloquial Chinese was freely used. Before that time, classical Chinese was the language taught to students. The difference between these two forms of Chinese is comparable to that between modern English and Chaucerian English. Classical Chinese was made especially difficult and was used as a tool by the elite. In other words, literacy was a sign of social status. Today the translation of classical Chinese is by and large an academic endeavor, whereas the translation of modern Chinese is used for practical purposes ranging from court translation to escorting visiting Chinese.

Regardless of what happens to the political fortunes of China, if Chinese is your language you can always go to Taiwan. This island just off the coast of mainland China's Fukien Province considers itself separate from the People's Republic and calls itself the Republic of China. Its government was established in 1949, when many mainland Chinese fled from the Communist takeover. In recent years its economic development has been spectacular, and it is an electronics and textile producer for the world.

Europe

When the European Community comes of age in 1992, opportunities will abound for those with language skills. Already in the United States there is a move to participate in the economic boom that is expected when Europe becomes a "nation" free of tariffs and other economic barriers.

At its inception in 1958, the European Economic Community, or Common Market, consisted of six countries: Belgium, France, the Federal Republic of Germany, Italy, Luxembourg, and the Netherlands, in a very loose economic federation. Since then six other countries have joined: Denmark, the Republic of Ireland, Great Britain, Greece, Portugal, and Spain.

Among the objectives of the European Community is to unify the currency, either by fixing the exchange rate or by having a "parallel Community currency." The Community also hopes to move toward a more unified foreign policy. Although many problems remain in standardizing economic practices, the EC uses the terms "coordination," "harmonization," and "integration" to describe its economic goals. As early as the 1970s it was contended that the advanced industrial countries of Europe were in an increasingly vulnerable position in the international market. Recent years have seen, according to the New York *Times*, "an explosion of cross-border investment," and "the emergence of a truly borderless market for capital" in Europe. According to scholar Helen Wallace, ". . . unified markets for goods, services, capital, and labor can improve levels of efficiency in production."

Clearly, it is to the advantage of American business to take part in this economic explosion. Companies are already moving to establish themselves in various European countries in order to share in the expected boom. This creates great opportunities for translators and interpreters at all levels in the business community to help smooth the transition from nationalist, independently operating companies to the multinational, interdependent forms in the EC. Business and social skills together with language skills will enable the economies of all the EC partners to thrive under these positive conditions.

Soviet Union

The historical relationship between the United States and the Soviet Union has long been one of fear and distrust, symbolized politically by the dueling and bargaining between American and Soviet leaders.

With the coming to power of Soviet President Mikhail Gorbachev a new sense of optimism came to permeate the scene as he began to introduce a multitude of reform programs simultaneously. The most difficult of these to approach was the Soviet economy. Although Americans tend to view the Soviet Union as a monolith, it is in fact a country of many minority nationalities. Gorbachev faces the necessity of finding a compromise between the nationalities' demands for less central government control and the reality that combining resources is the key to collective economic success.

Despite these continuing economic problems, Gorbachev's *perestroika*, or revolutionary restructuring of society, has permitted the creation of joint Soviet-American business ventures. As of mid-1989 some forty ventures with American companies or their foreign subsidiaries have been initiated. Perhaps the most widely advertised cultural exchange is in the beverage industry, where Pepsi kiosks now dot the streets of Soviet cities.

Glasnost, one of Gorbachev's slogans, can be defined as a political climate in which discussion of national problems is made possible by reduction in government censorship.

Despite these reforms, what Gorbachev calls "democracy" is different from our definition. Whereas we associate democracy with the consent of the majority, Gorbachev's democracy has more to do with a comprehensive program to transform society. He frequently uses the term "rethinking" as a catchword for social change, and he has said, "What we need is more dynamism, more social justice, more democracy—in a word, more socialism."

As a prospective interpreter or translator, you could find no better time than the present for learning Russian. At the university level, fourth-year Russian is being offered. As you will find, taking the fourth year of a language at a good university will permit you to read just about any kind of literature with the help of a dictionary, ranging from the newspaper to a novel.

English speakers who study Russian note the importance of inflection in the language. Inflection is the use of word endings that convey meaning. Whereas in English we use inflection to indicate whether an action is in the future, in progress, or completed, in Russian it is used even more frequently. Students also find something new in the use of the diminutive in a person's name, expressing the degree of intimacy or distance in one's relationship to that person.

Conclusion

With the enormous economic potential of all these wide-flung markets, the need for people who can communicate and carry on business in their languages is steadily increasing. The best opportunities exist for people who are trained in both business and language skills. Schools exist that train students specifically for international business. One such program is in operation at the Lauder Institute of the Wharton School, University of Pennsylvania, Philadelphia. It trains students for international management and education. Upon graduation students receive an MBA from the Wharton School and an MA from the School of International Studies.

The Institute enrolls fifty students for a consecutive twenty-four-month intensive training program. Applicants must have a baccalaureate degree from an accredited college and must score at the advanced level on the Oral Proficiency Interview of the American Council on the Teaching of Foreign Languages (ACTFL) scale. To graduate, they must progress from advanced to superior on that scale. During the first summer students work at an internship overseas, and the second summer as an international trainee overseas. The summer programs are given in Beijing, China (1989/90 Taipei, Taiwan); Osaka and Tokyo, Japan; Mexico City, Mexico; Caracas, Venezuela; São Paulo, Brazil; Paris, France; Munich, Germany, and Moscow, USSR.

Tuition is very expensive, but 80 percent of students receive financial aid either from the Lauder Institute, the Wharton School, or both.

Model Contract for Translators

The Translation Committee of PEN American Center has undertaken to secure the translator's status. They have prepared "A Handbook for Literary Translators," which includes important information each translator should know. You may acquire this pamphlet by writing to PEN American Center, 568 Broadway, New York, NY 10012. Here are a few excerpts including the MODEL CONTRACT taken from the pamphlet.

The translator is, in the Committee's view, a unique link between the original work and its audience in another language; his status as a collaborator with the original author should be recognized both by the publisher and the book's reader. One of the principal ways in which this recognition can be gained is by according translation the full status of a literary endeavor, and this recognition should begin with the agreement made between the translator and publisher.

The model contract we have drawn up represents an ideal toward which the Committee feels all translators should strive. But it is at present only this: an ideal. In today's marketplace, the provisions it contains are, in the great majority of cases, realized only in part. We feel, however, that translators should attempt to gain the inclusion of as many of them as possible.

The model contract and guidelines are based on the premise that the work in question is a work in copyright and that the translator is being engaged by the publisher to undertake the translation. In the translation of works in the public domain, the

Committee feels that the translator should be treated as an author and should receive the same contractual rights as an author.

MODEL CONTRACT

Contract of agreement made this day (date), between (translator's name), hereinafter called the Translator, and (publisher's name), hereinafter called the Publisher.

1. The Translator undertakes to translate (name of work and author) from (original language) into English. The Translator agrees to deliver to Publisher by (date of delivery) one clear, double-spaced copy of the completed translation of the work satisfactory for publication in the world market.

2. The translation should be a faithful rendition of the work into English; it shall neither omit anything from the original text nor add anything to it other than such verbal changes as are necessary in translating (original language) into English.

3. The Translator guarantees to the Publisher that no material of an objectionable or libelous character not present in the original work will be introduced into the translation. The Publisher in return will undertake to hold the Translator of the work harmless from all suits and all manner of claims and proceedings or expenses that may be taken against or incurred by them, on the grounds that the translation contains nothing objectionable or libelous which is not contained in the original work.

4. The Translator shall receive an advance (X dollars)* per thousand words of English text for the translation. The Translator will receive (X dollars)* upon signature of this contract by both parties, and the remainder due him will be paid upon delivery and acceptance of the completed translation.

5. The above sum shall be considered as an advance against a (X percent)* share of the royalties paid the original author, based on

the retail sales price of the hardcover edition based on net sales. The Translator shall also receive a (X percent)* share of the royalties due the original author on the earnings from any paperback edition and a prorated share of any subsidiary rights income due the original author accruing to him under the Publisher's agreement with him. The Translator will receive accounting statements from the Publisher under the same schedule as the original author.

6. Should the translation as submitted be deemed unsatisfactory by the Publisher, the Translator may ask that the translation be submitted to examination by a three-member panel of qualified translators, one member to be chosen by the Translator, one by the Publisher, and the third member by the two panel members thus designated. The costs of such arbitration will be borne by Publisher, and the panel's findings will be binding.

7. In the event the final translation is found to be unacceptable, the Translator shall receive one half of the remaining monies due him and the present contract will henceforward be deemed null and void.

8. The Translator shall be given the opportunity and reasonable time to examine and approve the copy-edited manuscript, as well as the galley proofs and page proofs of the translation, and to make any necessary changes therein, such approval not to be unreasonably withheld.

9. The translation will be copyrighted by the Publisher in the Translator's name, and the Translator hereby assigns his copyright to the Publisher for the term of the copyright, including renewals, granting the Publisher exclusive right to reproduce, publish, and sell the translation in whole or in part throughout the world.

10. All rights to their translation will revert to the Translator sixty days after the original author is notified by the Publisher that the book is declared out of print.

11. The Translator's name shall appear on the jacket and title page of the book and in all publicity and advertising copy for the book released by the Publisher.

In witness whereof, the parties hereto have signed this agreement at (place) on (date).

_____   _____

Translator's signature   Publisher's signature

_____

*4. The manner of payment may vary from contract to contract, but the Committee is strongly in favor of an advance payment on signature of approximately one third of the estimated total. At the present time, the work-for-hire fee per thousand words varies from very low amounts to as much as $60 or more in rare cases. The Committee feels that whereas a minimum $40 per thousand words has been the norm, $50 is perhaps closer to the present average. The translator should always ask for as much as he thinks he can get for a translation, but this minimum of $50 is strongly urged for the benefit of the professional as a whole.

*5. The matter of royalties is something no translator should fail to raise. In most European countries and Japan, the translator is entitled by law to royalties and automatically given them. the royalties to the translator are derived from those paid the original author under his agreement with the publisher. Such royalties are now generally a minimum 1.5 to 2 percent, or 15 to 20 percent of the author's royalties, and they rise at the same rate as the royalties paid to the original author.

ATA Accreditation

General Information

The American Translators Association (ATA), founded in 1959, is the largest professional society of translators and language specialists in the United States. It has over 2,300 members including free-lance and staff translators, translation users, translation service firms, and language teachers and students.

ATA's aims include advocating and promoting the recognition of translating as a profession, for mulating and maintaining standards of professional ethics, practices, and competence, and improving the standards and quality of translation. In 1963 the Accreditation Committee was established, and ATA began to offer tests in 1972. The purpose of the testing program is to accredit translators with the basic skills required to enter the free-lance market and to function as professionals in this field. Accreditation offers translators and clients one measurement of the translator's competence and commitment.

As of 1987 almost 900 translators are accredited ATA members. The certificate of accreditation becomes more valuable with every translator who acquires it and then gives proof of competence and professionalism.

Combinations Offered

Active and associate members of ATA may take an accreditation examination in any language pair offered. As of 1987, ATA offers tests in the following combinations:

French-English	English-French
German-English	English-German
Spanish-English	English-Spanish
Russian-English	English-Russian
Portuguese-English	English-Portuguese
Polish-English	English-Polish
Italian-English	English-Italian
Dutch-English	English-Dutch
Japanese-English.	

Test Dates

Accreditation tests are given at the annual ATA Convention in October, when new passages are introduced. Examination sittings nationwide are organized by local ATA chapters throughout the year and are announced in advance in the *ATA Chronicle*. Examinations can be given by special arrangements with ATA headquarters.

Fees

Accreditation is offered as a nonprofit service to ATA members. The full fee covers the costs of two or three graders, administrative support, proctoring, room rental, and postage. The fee for each accreditation examination is $50. The fee for the first retest in the same language combination is $30; the full fee is charged for subsequent retests. Candidates must be active or associate ATA members who have paid their annual membership dues of $50 ($25 student) or joined ATA before taking the test.

The Accreditation Examination

The ATA accreditation examination is an open-book, three-hour test. Accreditation examinations in all language combinations consist of five passages, one in each of the following categories: general, literary, legal or business, scientific or medical, and semitechnical.

Candidates are expected to complete three passages of their choice within three hours, proceeding at their own pace.

Dictionaries

Dictionaries and reference materials are permitted during the examination. Dictionaries are the professional translator's tools of the trade, and small pocket dictionaries are not adequate for the accreditation examination. Candidates are advised to use comprehensive dictionaries, such as the well-known Collins, Cassell's, and Larousse series, together with specialized business, legal, and technical dictionaries.

Some of the most comprehensive dictionaries include:

French

Harrap's *New Standard French and English Dictionary*

Spanish

Simon ans Schuster's *International Dictionary*
Robb, *Dictionary of Modern Business*
Collazo, *Encyclopedic Dictionary of Technical Terms*

Portuguese

Taylor, *A Portuguese-English Dictionary Novo Michaelis, Dicionario Ilustrado/The New Michaelis Illustrated Dictionary*, Melhoramentos

Italian

Sansoni-Harrap's *Dictionary of the Italian and English Languages*

German

Harrap's *German-English Dictionary* (3 fo 4 volumes published)
Langenscheidt, *New Muret-Sanders Encyclopedic Dictionary*

DeVries and Hermann, *German-English Technical and Engineering Dictionary*, 2d edition

Ernst, *German-English Dictionary of Engineering and Technology*, 4th edition

Russian

Smirnitskiy, *Russian-English Dictionary*

The Oxford *Russian-English Dictionary*

Kuznetsov, *Russian-English Polytechnical Dictionary*

Bol'shoy Anglo-russkiy slovar (2 vols), publ

Sovetskaya entsiklopediya (English-Russian)

Callaham Russian-English *Technical and Chemical Dictionary*

Polish

Stanislawski *Wielki Slownik Polsko-Angielski Kosciuszko Foundation Dictionary Slownik naukowo-techniczny polsko-angielski*

Japanese

Nelson, Andrew. *A Modern Reader's Japanese-English Character Dictionary*

Kenkyusha's *Japanese-English Dictionary*

Local chapters are urged to provide an unabridged English dictionary in the examination room, and candidates are advised to bring a target-language dictionary to check for spelling, diacritical marks, optimal word choices, and universal vocabulary (words spelled similarly in source and target language that may not be included in a bilingual dictionary). While candidates should work independently, occasionally reference materials may be consulted separately by several translators with the prior knowledge and permission of the proctor.

Standards

Translation requires research and analytical ability, knowledge of the source language, editing skills, and the ability to write well in the target language. The goal is an accurate, idiomatic, edited translation, without additions or omissions, adhering closely to the text, that is ready for typing and then use or publication without further revision.

Grading Practices

Accreditation examinations are graded independently by two or three graders who know the candidate only by number. Two major errors in substance or one major error and six or seven minor errors per passage mean failure in that passage. The results are determined when two graders concur that two passages out of three merit a passing or failing grade. If the first two graders do not concur, a third grader receives unmarked copies of the disputed passages and breaks the tie. Since the results are reached by impartial consensus there is no appeals process; instead candidates are offered one retest at below cost. The graders tend to be established staff and free-lance translators, some with university affiliations, who were selected because of their outstanding performance on the accreditation examination.

Major errors include: *major mistranslations* where the intent of the original is completely lost, *omissions* of essential materials (including titles, paragraph numbers), *additions* of extraneous material, serious *grammatical errors* in the use of the target language, and *dissimilar alternative translations.*

Minor errors include: *minor mistranslations* that convey some of the original meaning, *unidiomatic usage, awkwardness, insignificant omissions, spelling and punctuation errors*, and *similar alternative translations.*

Units of measurement should not be converted.

Candidates are not penalized for inability to translate words not contained in their dictionaries. They should write the *original term* and a note stating that it is not in their sources.

High-Risk Candidates

Candidates attempting to translate from their mother tongue into a foreign language or lacking practical translating experience are at a high risk of failure. With the rare exception of individuals raised in bilingual households or educated abroad, such candidates should take a practice test before attempting the accreditation examination.

Practice Test Program

The practice test is an actual test passage from a previous accreditation examination which is graded with comments by a committee graders. The fee is $7.50 per examination. Write to:

Examination Procedures

Candidates should arrive at the examination room on time with writing instruments that copy well (dark ink or soft pencil). Paper will be provided. Time will be required before the examination to handle administrative details, distribute test packets, and review instructions. Candidates must have three full hours in which to complete the examination. They may leave the room at any time during this period. Completed examinations must be handed to the proctor in sealed envelopes bearing the signature and address of the candidate. Scrap paper must be included to ensure confidentiality (it will not be forwarded to the graders). Candidates should not waste time recopying their translations; legible deletions and insertions are acceptable. Extra time should be used for proofreading and checking for omissions.

The proctors may organize the examination sitting at their discretion to ensure that the candidates work independently and undisturbed. Smoking is not permitted unless a separate smoking room is provided. Special arrangements are permitted for the handicapped with specific approval of the accreditation committee chairman.

The accreditation examination is not a teaching tool and becomes the exclusive property of the committee. The examination will not be returned, and the results will not be discussed. Candidates are required to sign a statement of their acceptance of this rule on the examination envelope.

Results may be expected in approximately three months.

All correspondence about the accreditation examination program should be addressed to:

Accreditation Committee
American Translators Association
109 Croton Avenue
Ossining, NY 10562

Sample Résumés

PEDRO VASQUEZ
1021 Amsterdam Avenue
New York, NY 10025
(212) 963-1070

OBJECTIVE	Editor or Assistant Editor, domestic or international
EDUCATION	BA, University of Wisconsin Major: Political Science 1980 Columbia University, New York Doctoral candidate La Sorbonne, Paris, France Certificat Supérieur de Langue 1988
WORK EXPERIENCE	McGraw-Hill Co., New York *Editor of Trade Magazine* (Approved editorial content, organized and balanced advertising space with resulting increase in advertising revenue of 18% 1984–present

Architectural Digest, Boulder, Colorado
Translator and Editor in New York
office
(Translated French and Spanish editorial
material into English, selected photographs, and edited for publication)   1984

Mainstream Publsihngn Co., New York
Translator
(Translated from English into French for
all out going material to launch international information service. Translated
from Spanish to English, Source Book on
Spanish Architecture)   1982

Jovanovich and Spear, New York
Editorial Consultant
(Consusltant in preparation of books on
conversational Spanish and French) 1980

LANGUAGES	French and Spanish (excellent), Italian (fair)
TRAVEL	Extensive travel throughout Europe, South America and the U.S.
PERSONAL (optional)	Born: December 29, 1958 Health: Excellent Single
REFERENCES	Available on request

30 Fifth Avenue   Home (212) 567-3428
New York, NY 10003   Office (212) 555-3366

ELOISE K. MILLER

OBJECTIVE:	Career in International Banking
	EXPERIENCE
CREDIT ANALYST:	*1980–Present* Chase Manhattan Bank, New York, NY. Worked on Sovereign Risk analysis for Latin American area. As a result of my analysis, Chase Manhattan was able to increase profits in Peru and Venezuela.
RUSSIAN INTERPRETER:	*Summers 1978, 1979* Detroit Auto Fair Accompanied and interpreted for Russian dignitaries during their stay in Detroit.
EDUCATION:	*MBA,* Wharton School of Business, University of Pennsylvania, Philadelphia, Pennsylvania, 1980. *BA,* University of Michigan, Ann Arbor, Michigan. Double major in Russian and Spanish, 1978.
ASSOCIATIONS:	American Association of Translators and Interpreters University of Michigan Club of New York
LANGUAGES:	Fluent in Spanish and Russian.
PERSONAL:	Age 29, single, excellent health.
REFERENCES:	Available on request.

Appendix D

Selected Reading

Aitken, D.J., ed. *World List of Universities*, 16th ed. International Association of Universities, 1985.

Akmajian, Adrian, et al. *Linguistics: An Introduction to Language and Communication*, 2d ed., MIT Press, Boston, 1984.

Ayers, B. Drummond, Jr. "A New Breed of Diplomat." *The New York Times Magazine*, September 11, 1983.

Bourgoin, Edward. *Foreign Languages and Your Career*, 3d ed. Columbia Language Services, Washington, DC, 1984.

Cassidy, Maggie Brown. *Taking Students Abroad.* Pro Lingua Associates, 15 Elm Street, Brattleboro, VT 05301, 1988.

Congrat-Butler, Stefan. *Translation and Translators: An International Directory and Guide*, R.R. Bowker Order Department, P.O. Box 1807, Ann Arbor, MI 48106.

Crump, Ted. *Translators and Translations in the Federal Government: A Spot Check*, 2719 Colston Drive, Chevy Chase, MD 20815.

Huebener, Dr. Theodore. *Opportunities in Foreign Language Careers.* Vocational Guidance Manuals, Inc., Courier-Journal and Louiville Times Co., 1975.

Kocher, Eric. *International Jobs: Where They Are and How to Get Them.* Addison-Wesley Publishing Co., Inc., 1 Jacob Way, Reading, MA 01867, revised 1984.

Krawutschke, Peter W., ed. *Translator and Interpreter Training and Foreign Language Pedagogy.* Center for Research in Translation, State University of New York at Binghamton, Binghamton, NY 13901, 1989.

Larson, Mildred L. *Meaning-Based Translation*. University Press of America, 4720 Boston Way, Lanham, MD 20706, 1984.

Newmark, Peter. *Approaches to Translation*. Pergamon Press Ltd., Prentice-Hall Inc., Englewood Cliffs, NJ 07632, 1981

Overseas Employment Opportunities for Educators. Department of Defense, Overseas Dependents Schools, 2461 Eisenhower Avenue, Alexandria, VA 22331.

Seleskovitch, Danica. *Interpreting for International Conferences*. Pen and Booth Publishing, 1608 R Street, NW, Washington, DC 20009.

Survey of Schools Offering Translator and Interpreter Training. ATA Translation Studies Committee, American Translators Association, 109 Croton Avenue, Ossining, NY 10562.

Webster, Stever. *Teach Overseas 1948–1985: The Educator's World-Wide Handbook and Directory to International Teaching in Overseas Schools, Colleges and Universities*, Maple Tree Publishing Co., Publishing Co., P.O. Box 479, General Post Office, NY 10116, 1985.

Appendix **E**

List of the Specialized Agencies of the United Nations and Other Related International Organizations

FAO   Food and Agriculture Organization
            Via delle Terme di Caracalla
            00100 Rome, Italy

            For applications from the United States
            FAO Liaison Office
            One United Nations Plaza
            Room DC1-1125
            New York, NY 10017

GATT   General Agreement on Tariffs and Trade Centre
            William Rappard
            154 Rue de Lausanne
            1211 Geneva 21, SWITZERLAND

IAEA   International Atomic Energy Agency
            Vienna International Center
            Wargramer Strasse 5
            A-1400, Vienna, AUSTRIA

IBRD   International Bank for Reconstruction and
            Development (World Bank)
            1818 "H" Street, NW
            Washington, DC 20433

ICAO	International Civil Aviation Organization P.O. Box 400 Succursale: Place de l'Aviation Internationale 1000 Sherbrooke Street West Montreal, Quebec, CANADA 2H3A 2R2
IDA	International Development Association (World Bank) 1818 ''H'' Street, NW Washington, DC 20433
IFAD	International Fund for Agricultural Development Via del Serafico 107 00142 Rome, ITALY
IFC	International Finance Corporation (World Bank) 1818 ''H'' Street, NW Washington, DC 20433
ILO	International Labour Organisation 4, route des Morillons CH-1211 Geneva 22, SWITZERLAND For applicants from the United States Washington Branch 1750 New York Avenue, NW Washington, DC 20006
IMO	International Maritime Organization 4 Albert Embankment London SE1 7SR, UNITED KINGDOM
IMF	International Monetary Fund 700 19th Street, NW Washington, DC 20431
ITU	International Telecommunication Union Palais des Nations 1211 Geneva 10, SWITZERLAND

UNCTAD	United Nations Conference on Trade and Development Palais des Nations 1211 Geneva 10, SWITZERLAND
UNDP	United Nations Development Programme Division of Information One United Nations Plaza New York, NY 10017
UNDRO	Office of the United Nations Disaster Relief Co-Ordinator Palais des Nations 1211 Geneva 10, SWITZERLAND
UNEP	United Nations Environment Programme P.O. Box 30552 Nairobi, KENYA
UNESCO	United Nations Educational, Scientific and Cultural Organization UNESCO House 7, Place de Fontenoy 75700 Paris, FRANCE
UNFPA	United Nations Fund for Population Activities 220 East 42nd Street, 19th Floor New York, NY 10017
UNHCR	United Nations Commissioner for Refugees Liaison Office United Nations New York, NY 10017
UNICEF	United Nations Children's Fund UNICEF House New York, NY 10017

UNIDO   United Nations Industrial Development
        Organization
        Liaison Office
        United Nations
        New York, NY 10017

UNITAR   United Nations Institute for Training and Research
        United Nations
        New York, NY 10017

UNRWA   United Nations Relief and Works Agency for
        Palestine Refugees
        Liaison Office
        United Nations
        New York, NY 10017

UNU   United Nations University Headquarters
        Toho Seimei Building
        15-1 Shibuya 2-chome, Shibuya-ku
        Tokyo 150, JAPAN

UPU   Union Postale Universelle
        Weltpostrasse 4
        3000 Berne 15, SWITZERLAND

WHO   World Health Organization
        20 Avenue Appia
        1211 Geneva 27, SWITZERLAND

        For applicants from the Americas and Canada
        Regional Office for the Americas
        525 23rd Street, NW
        Washington, DC 20037

WIPO   World Intellectual Property Organization
        34, Chemin des Colombettes
        1211 Geneva, SWITZERLAND

WMO   World Meteorological Organization
                41, Avenue Giuseppe-Motta
                Geneva, SWITZERLAND

UNRISD   United Nations Research Institute for
                Social Development
                Palais des Nations
                1211 Geneva 10, SWITZERLAND

Test Samples

For government positions you need to complete Standard Form 171, Application for Federal employment. This general application form, which asks for background information, can be obtained by writing to your state Office of Personnel Management.

To apply for a position as a Translator/Précis-writer for the United Nations, you must first fill out a standard application form (which is necessary for all U.N. jobs) and then take a two-day written examination. This exam usually consists of four papers: (1) Translation into applicant's main language of an English text of a general nature, except in the case of English translator/précis-writers who must translate a French text of a general nature (three hours); (2) Summary in the applicant's main language of an English statement, except in the case of English translators/précis-writers, who must summarize a French statement (two hours); (3) Translation into the applicant's main language of two texts chosen from a total of five specialized English texts, except for English translators/précis-writers, who translate from French (three hours); (4) Translation into the applicant's main language of any two texts chosen from eight texts offered in the other four official languages (i.e., other than the applicant's main language and the language of papers (1), (2) and (3) above (two hours).

After successful completion of the written exam, applicants are interviewed by a Board of Examiners.

Escort Interpreter applicants to the State Department are first interviewed on their educational and professional experiences and their language(s) exposure. Applicants are also asked questions about current events, general interests, American institutions and lifestyles, economic trends, the labor movement, civil rights, etc. The applicant is then expected to complete a consecutive interpreting exercise—the interviewer improvises a passage in English lasting two to three minutes, and the applicant, who takes notes, is expected to render the passage. Finally, there may be an exercise in simultaneous interpreting. The test/interview usually takes an hour.

The Foreign Service Exam is taken by Foreign Service Officer applicants. If the applicant is successful on the exam, he or she goes on to an all-day oral assessment consisting of an oral exam with two examiners, a written essay prepared in 45 minutes on an assigned topic, a written summary exercise, a two-part group exercise consisting of a presention of a proposal and a negotiating session, and a written In-Basket exam in which the applicant deals with a series of problems and situations.

The Foreign Service Exam is divided into two sections of multiple choice questions—General Background Questions about everything from management to economics, and English Expression Questions on grammar, vocabulary, and comprehension—and takes half a day.

Here are four sample questions:

General Background

Objective: To measure your understanding of the problem of economic growth.

1)   A high level of industrialization has generally been accompanied by
     (A) greater interdependence of various sectors of the society
     (B) a rigidity in the class structure
     (C) lessening of competition for scarce commodities and resources
     (D) increased demands for animate sources of power

Objective: To measure your awareness of the role of ethnic minorities in the development of political attitudes in the United States.

2) W.E.B. Du Bois led the early 20th-century reaction against the doctrines of Booker T. Washington on the grounds that blacks should
    (A) repatriate themselves to Africa
    (B) demand their full constitutional rights
    (C) seek to win a place in American society through vocational training
    (D) remain in rural areas rather than be encouraged to migrate to cities

ENGLISH EXPRESSION QUESTIONS

3) Although Newfoundlands are large, and in appearance even awesome, it would be difficult to find dogs with gentler dispositions than them.
    No error.

4) The ambassador became ill after eating at the restaurant, but she did not sue the management.
    Omit *but*

    Your rewritten sentence will begin with which of the following?
    (A) Since the
    (B) Although
    (C) When becoming
    (D) Even if becoming
    (E) After eating

Answers: 1)A, 2)B, 3)D, 4)B

Index